The Eagle

"Don't Despair" Passages In The Gospel Of John

Ron Lavin

CSS Publishing Company, Inc., Lima, Ohio

THE EAGLE

Copyright © 2008 by
CSS Publishing Company, Inc.
Lima, Ohio

Unless otherwise marked, scripture quotations are from the Holy Bible, New International Version. Copyright © 1973, 1978, 1984 International Bible Society. Used by permission of Zondervan Bible Publishers. All rights reserved.

Scripture quotations marked (RSV) are from the Revised Standard Version of the Bible,
copyrighted 1946, 1952 ©, 1971, 1973, by the Division of Christian Education of the
National Council of the Churches of Christ in the USA. Used by permission.

Scripture quotations marked (NEB) are from the New English Bible. Copyright © the Del-
egates of the Oxford University Press and the Syndics of the Cambridge University Press,
1961, 1970. Reprinted by permission.

Scripture quotations marked (NRSV) are from the New Revised Standard Version of the
Bible, copyright 1989 by the Division of Christian Education of the National Council of the
Churches of Christ in the USA. Used by permission.

Scripture quotations marked (KJV) are from the King James Version of the Bible, in the
public domain.

Scripture quotations marked (Phillips) are from The New Testament in Modern English,
J. B. Phillips translation, copyright © 1958, 1959, 1960 J. B. Phillips and 1947, 1952,
1955, 1957 The Macmillan Company, New York. Used by permission. All rights reserved.

Library of Congress Cataloging-in-Publication Data

Lavin, Ronald J.
    The eagle : "don't despair" passages in the Gospel of John / Ron Lavin.
      p. cm.
    Includes bibliographical references.
    ISBN 0-7880-2555-4 (perfect bound : alk. paper)
    1. Bible. N.T. John—Textbooks. 2. Consolation—Biblical teaching—Textbooks. 3.
Encouragement—Biblical teaching—Textbooks. I. Title.

BS2615.C584L38 2008
226.5'06—dc22

2008018706

For more information about CSS Publishing Company resources, visit our website at
www.csspub.com or email us at csr@csspub.com or call (800) 241-4056.

Cover design by Ron Lavin and Barbara Spencer
ISBN-13: 978-0-7880-2555-6
ISBN-10: 0-7880-2555-4   PRINTED IN USA

Dedicated to

Vonda Kay Younker

and her parents, Walt and Carolyn Younker

and

Sara Franing

and her parents, Dick and Judith Franing

Books By Ron Lavin

The Four Gospels Series
The Eagle ("Don't Despair" Passages In The Gospel Of John)

Evangelization
Witness (The Reign Of God And Missional Churches Today)

The Another Look Series
Only The Lonely (Another Look At Loneliness)
People Who Met Jesus (Another Look At The Suffering, Death, And Resurrection Of The Lord)
The Big Ten (Another Look At The Ten Commandments)
Saving Grace (Another Look At The Word And The Sacraments)
Abba (Another Look At The Lord's Prayer)
Stories To Remember (Another Look At The Parables Of Jesus)
I Believe; Help My Unbelief (Another Look At The Apostles' Creed)

Published Sermons
Sermons On The Gospels, Series II, Cycle C (Eleven sermons by Ron Lavin)
Sermons On The First Readings, Series II, Cycle B (Fifteen sermons by Ron Lavin)
Numerous other published sermons in six other volumes of sermons

Other Books
Turning Griping Into Gratitude
Empty Spaces; Empty Places (written with Constance Sorenson)
Way To Grow! (Dynamic Church Growth Through Small Groups)
The Advocate
The Great I AM
Previews Of Coming Attractions
Alone/Together
You Can't Start A Car With A Cross
Roots And Wings
You Can Grow In A Small Group

A Strategy For Renewal
The Human Chain For Divine Grace (editor)
Jesus In Stained Glass
Jesus Christ, The Liberator (written with Bill Grimmer, MD)
Hey, Mom, Look At Me!

Table Of Contents

Foreword

It is often true that when life unloads heavy burdens upon us we turn to the Bible for much-needed comfort. As a seasoned pastor, I know that even those who have never looked inside the cover of their family Bibles will try to locate some help for their grief and sadness and depression. Our Bible is very sure about the comfort it offers when life tumbles. Jesus promised the disciples in his Beatitudes, "Blessed are those who mourn, for they shall be comforted" (Matthew 5:4). Saint Paul wrote it this way: "Blessed be the God and Father of our Lord Jesus Christ, the Father of mercies and the God of all consolation, who consoles us in all our affliction, so that we might be able to console those who are in any affliction ..." (1 Corinthians 1:3-4).

Comfort In The Old Testament

There are many examples of despair in the Old Testament, mainly when there is mourning for the death of loved ones. The Hebrew word for comfort at a time like this is probably best described as "to console." Consider these examples: Ruth's comfort of Naomi in her sorrow and the comfort that Ruth receives from Boaz (Ruth 2:13). When Isaac's mother died, Rebekah comforted him (Genesis 24:67). David consoled Bathsheba upon the demise of her son (2 Samuel 12:24).

According to the psalms, comfort for our affliction is through knowing and believing in God's promises, "This is my comfort in my distress, that your promise gives me life" (Psalm 119:50). There are also passages that designate a physical refreshment (Genesis 18:5; Proverbs 11:25). In the Old Testament, I liked best the changes in the sufferer's situation that replaces sorrow with joy and thus moves us away from despair (Isaiah 40:1, 2; 49:13; 51:3, 12, 19; 61:2; 66:13).

In Israel's scriptures, God is often portrayed as a God of compassion, mercy, and pity (2 Samuel 24:14; Isaiah 63:15; Psalm 24:6). There is even a claim that the rhythm of the verbiage of the comfort theme in Isaiah has its soothing influence. "Comfort, O comfort my people, says your God. Speak tenderly to Jerusalem ..." (Isaiah 40:1-2).

When we read of Job's need for a remedy for despair, we read of the likes of Eliphas, Bildad, and Zophar, whose attempts at giving comfort were, at best, misguided attempts, and at worst, the cruel making of Job's agony much worse (Job 2:11). It is a lesson for us on how *not* to give comfort in a time of despair, which we all need to learn.

Comfort In The New Testament

In the New Testament, we find the Greek word for comfort most often is *paraklesis* (occurring over 100 times), which literally means "a calling to one's side." That is the way out of threatened despair. Newer renditions of the Greek tend toward translating the word *paraklesis* as "counselor." I hope we will insist in the future that comforter not be forgotten. Jesus was definite of profound comfort to Mary by crying with her at the death of her brother, Lazarus, in John 11:33-36. This plaintiveness of Jesus infects the lives of believers and gives strong meaning to Paul's words: "Blessed be God and Father of the Lord Jesus Christ, the father of mercies and the God of all consolation, who consoles us in our affliction ..." (2 Corinthians 1:4-5).

Through one's congregation we can gain, and also give to each other, help in times of despair. Paul wrote to his Thessalonian Christians: "Therefore encourage one another ... encourage one another and build up each other, as indeed you are doing" (1 Thessalonians 4:18; 5:11). Ron Lavin illustrates this principle elegantly in the following chapters as he examines the passages in John' gospel concerning the admonition to not despair.

Luke, in Acts 20:12 and Paul, in 2 Corinthians 7:13, talk about being comforted by God. That says much to us about what our ministries, lay and clergy, ought to be about. We live in an age of much pain, depression, despair, and hurt. Our ministry is to be comforting to all those who are suffering.

As you read *The Eagle*, you will see that the concept of comfort for despair is multifaceted. Already mentioned is the comfort of those in any affliction, those in need of renewal, replacing sorrow with joy, having a soothing effect, and from the congregation. To these we must add Paul's idea that God comforts/consoles the downcast (2 Corinthians 7:6). And we gain relief from despair in reading the scripture and from Christian fellowship. These add still more advice as to what our discipleship ought to be about as an individual and as a congregation.

A Great Example

In Acts 4:36 we learn of an excellent example of a man who must have been exceptionally sensitive to people's needs around him for help out of despair. He was a Levite by the original name of Joseph to whom the apostles gave the name of Barnabas, which means "son of encouragement." What a marvelous name for a believer! There are a number of those who could be renamed Barnabas in the following chapters of this book. The writer of John wrote about them and Ron Lavin has written about them as well. Any congregation would be abundantly blessed to have Barnabases in their fellowship of hurting, almost despairing, believers. And it is essential that we who preach the Good News be as "Barnabas" in our message as well!

Just reading the scripture can also give much-needed solace. Paul, no stranger to adversity and pain, wrote to the church in Rome, "... so by steadfastness and by the encouragement of the scriptures we might have hope" (Romans 15:4b).

Us old-timers who have already lived a long life in Christ know the spiritual lift that we have sought, and obtained, from Christian fellowship. Saint Paul again (this time he is writing to Philemon) says, "I have indeed received much joy and encouragement from your love, because the hearts of the saints have been refreshed through you, my brother" (Philemon 7).

Paul uses the word *paraklesis* ten times in 2 Corinthians. Sometimes this letter has been referred to as the letter of comfort. It always means much more to be passive, patient, and accepting of the pain and struggle; it relates to us gaining strength through maintaining and undergirding the power of the Holy Spirit. I have found

11

that God most comforts/encourages me when I am comforting/encouraging others.

Encouragement From Our Hymn Singing
Johannes Olearius wrote the following words in 1671 to be sung to the familiar hymn tune *Nun danket alle Gott.* When on the edge of despair we can sing it yet today. Hymn singing often will cheer our hearts and encourage our despairing souls.

> *The Lord, my God, be praised, my hope, my life from*
> *   heaven,*
> *The spirit, whom the Son in love to me hath given.*
> *'Tis he revives my heart, 'tis he that gives me pow'r,*
> *Help, comfort, and support in sorrow's gloomy hour.*

John quotes Jesus as saying to his disciples reassuring words such as, "Do not let your hearts be troubled...." Lavin covers the rest John has to say on the subject very well. Do not despair and do read on.

Jerry L. Schmalenberger
Retired President, Pacific Lutheran Seminary,
    Berkeley, California

A Word About The Four Gospels Series

The four gospels give us an overview of the life of Jesus Christ from four different perspectives. These four gospels are more like portraits than photographs. In writing books on the four gospels, I have discovered and rediscovered the uniqueness, richness, and depth of each of the portraits. My hope is that readers of these books will make their own discoveries of the unlimited treasures of the greatest story ever told.

The first book in the four-book series is *The Eagle ("Don't Despair" Passages In The Gospel Of John)*. The world places a big "No exit" sign over life. The high-flying eagle, a symbol for both Jesus and John, represents getting a high perspective on what is happening to us in life and death. Despair and suffering without hope is the theme that many in the world preach. This theme is reversed by the fourth gospel. There is always a way out — even a way out of death.

The second book in the series is *The Servant Lord (Challenging And Encouraging Passages In The Gospel Of Mark)*. The paradox of Jesus as servant and Lord is examined. On the one hand, Jesus is the authoritative and powerful ruler of all, facing down the powers of evil. On the other hand, Jesus is the servant of all, giving his life as a ransom (Mark 10:45). Both challenges and encouragement spring from this paradox.

The third book will be *The Divine Physician (Life-Saving Prescriptions In The Gospel Of Luke)*. As a doctor, Luke's portrait includes details of the birth, life, death, and resurrection of Jesus. As a historian, Luke tells an orderly account of Jesus' life. As a missionary, Luke is concerned with Jesus' outreach to all people, including women and children. As a Greek, Luke shows Jesus' outreach to lost sinners and outcasts like the prodigal son (Luke 15:11-32).

The fourth book will be *The King And His Kingdom (The Cost Of Discipleship In The Gospel Of Matthew)*. Matthew, the former tax collector and record keeper, shares his memories of the Sermon on the Mount and other teachings of the Lord, as well as events in the Lord's life. Discipleship is pictured as going through the eye of the needle, a door in the walls of Jerusalem, the holy city.

The high-flying eagle represents John because in his narrative he rises to the loftiest heights in dealing with the mind of Christ and the life of a Christian.

Introduction

Sister Celica was sitting by a window in her convent one day when she was handed a letter from home. Upon opening it, a $20 bill dropped out. She was most pleased at receiving the gift from her folks, but as she read the letter, her attention was distracted by the actions of a shabbily dressed stranger who was leaning against a post in front of the convent.

She couldn't get him off her mind, and thinking that he might be in financial difficulties, she took the $20 bill and wrapped it in a piece of paper on which she wrote: "Don't despair." She signed the note: Sister Celica, put it in an envelope and threw it out the window. It landed at the vagrant's feet. He picked it up, read the message, looked at the twenty and then looked at the nun with a puzzled expression. Tipping his hat, he went off down the street.

The next day Sister Celica was in her cell praying when she was told that some man was at the convent door, insisting that he talk to her. When she got to the door, the vagrant handed her $200 in rolled up bills.

"Why? What's this for?" she asked.

"Your horse, 'Don't Despair,' paid ten to one at the race track," he replied.

When you believe the message, "Don't despair," it pays more than ten to one. Believing that message from Jesus Christ pays eternal benefits in this life and the next.

"Don't despair," is the message of Jesus in the gospel of John. Despair is suffering without hope. People who have read this gospel over the years have repeatedly been encouraged to see their suffering from a higher perspective. Therefore, hope has been found or rediscovered in the fourth gospel.

The fourth gospel opens with the announcement that Jesus (God's Word) became flesh and made his dwelling among us. Since we know that God identifies with us in all of our suffering, we have hope, no matter what life brings us. Even in facing the death of a loved one or our own death, we are invited not to despair.

The most famous passage in the fourth gospel is John 3:16: "For God so loved the world that he gave his one and only Son, that whoever believes in him shall not perish but have eternal life." God's Son died on the cross for each of us as if there were only one of us. That's why we are told, "Don't despair."

John 14:1-2 encourages us not to despair. Jesus says, "Do not let your hearts be troubled. Trust in God, trust also in me. In my Father's house are many rooms; if it were not so, I would have told you. I am going there to prepare a place for you." Then Jesus adds, "I will not leave you as orphans" (John 14:18 NIV). Other translations read: "I will not leave you desolate" (RSV); "I will not leave you bereft" (NEB); and "I am not going to leave you alone" (Phillips). That's why we do not lose hope. Whatever we have to face, we do not face it alone. "In this world you will have trouble. But take heart! I have overcome the world" (John 16:33). In other words, "Don't despair."

16

The gospel of John is filled with encouraging words about Jesus being present with us in all our suffering. When he comes, he overcomes the world's troubles, bringing love, light, and life to whatever situation we face. The flashing neon light "No exit" that seems to be hanging over many human situations is an illusion. In the fourth gospel we hear Jesus say there is a way out: "I am the way, the truth, and the life" (John 14:6). That's the eagle's eye view of our situations.

Some situations seem hopeless. There seems to be no way out of the suffering we or loved ones are going through. "Hold on. I'll show you the way," Jesus says. "I am the way."

Some years ago, I spoke on the gospel of John at a week of meetings on spiritual renewal at a Methodist church camp in northern Iowa. One morning as I arrived at breakfast, I noticed a young father and mother and their little girl sitting at a table alone. As I approached, I asked if I might join them. "Sure," they said. "We'd be glad to have you sit with us." As I began to sit down, I noticed that the little girl's eyes were shut. "Your daughter must be very sleepy," I said smiling, trying to start off the conversation on a light note. "She's still got her eyes closed."

"Her eyes aren't closed," the father said. "She has no eyes."

My apologies were accepted graciously, but I felt like a fool. "It was a natural mistake," the mother said as she noticed my discomfort. Then she shared the story. "We were really troubled when our daughter was born without eyes, but our faith in Jesus got us through. Our daughter's name is Vonda Kay. She was named after a Miss America, because she was such a beautiful baby. She still is," the mother said. Vonda Kay smiled.

"Don't you and Vonda Kay get discouraged?" I asked.

"We get discouraged from time to time," the father said, "but we are never without hope, just like you said in the lecture yesterday. Whenever we approach despair, we just think about how God sent his Son into the world to save us. That gets us through every time. That God loved us enough to send his Son gives us a higher perspective on what has happened. That's what you told us in your talk about the gospel of John, isn't it?"

17

"I may have said the words in my presentation," I replied, "but you folks are living the words. You are an inspiration." We ate our meals together for the remainder of the conference. We became friends. I was the lecturer, but they were the wise teachers of the love, light, and life Jesus promised to those who believe him.

That's what I call faith.

Another Christian family had to deal with a problem so huge it would wipe out most parents. Their daughter Sara was born with teratoma, a rare massive tumor on the right side of her face and neck. It was four and a half times the size of her head. The prognosis was brutal: imminent death without surgery. With surgery, there was only 1% chance of survival. Hopeless? It certainly appeared so. Despair? Who wouldn't respond that way? Yet, Dick and Judith Franing clung by their fingernails to their faith in the Lord.

Dick and Judith had an eagle's eye view of what was happening to them and their baby. Isaiah 40:30-31 says it well: "They who wait for the Lord shall renew their strength, they shall mount up on wings like eagles, they shall run and not be weary, they shall walk and not faint." That's the high perspective that got the Franings through the difficult days right after Sara's birth with a huge tumor on her face.

It's not what happens to us that determines how we come out, but how we respond to what happens to us. The Franings responded with faith in God. They didn't just respond from a human point of view. They got up high and tried to see things from God's point of view. They didn't understand what was happening, but they knew that God understood and they trusted him. They didn't know the answers, but they knew the One who did know the answers. They waited for the Lord. They were up on the wings of eagles.

Sara survived that massive surgery and 35 more reconstructive surgeries to help with her facial deformity. She graduated from college. Today she plays the piano, violin, and cello. She works in Cleveland, in functional electrical stimulation, helping people with spinal cord injuries and other similar limitations. She has a deep trust in the Lord. She works in her church teaching Sunday school and caring for the older members of her congregation.

Sara's parents, Dick and Judith Franing, described their journey from darkness to light like this: "Throughout it all we have called upon the Lord for strength and he has answered our prayers."

Sara expresses her perspective on hard times like this: "Hard times are those stepping stones that I must stay on top of and not fall in between the cracks."

Since I was their pastor when the Franings went through this ordeal, they recently sent me an update on what has happened in Sara's life. They also sent Sara's unpublished manuscript called *Lucky Pennies*, the story of all the people who have encouraged her in the faith journey of love, light, and life. One of those people is President Jimmy Carter, with whom Sara worked in Americus, Georgia, on Habitat for Humanity.

Clearly, Sara, Dick, and Judith Franing live out the creed of the gospel of John: "You are not alone. There is love, light, and life (the eternal kind) for all situations, even those that from a human perspective look bleak." They have gained an eagle's eye view of what happens to us in life.

The symbol for the gospel of John is an eagle. Like a high-flying eagle, John sees things as they are, not as they seem to be. What most people consider reality — the view from this world — is not what the fourth gospel pictures as reality. The reality of eternity helps the readers of John's gospel to gain a perspective on what is troubling them. The illusions of this world are called darkness in the first chapter of John. The light is Christ. "The light shines in the darkness, but the darkness has not understood it" (John 1:5).

We are encouraged to let the light of Christ shine around us and within us. We are called to fly like an eagle and to have that kind of higher perspective, which comes only from faith in Christ. Instead, too often, we just feel sorry for ourselves as we think of ourselves as limited creatures. We often act like chickens instead of eagles.

Consider this parable.

> *While walking through a forest, a farmer found a young eagle. He took it home and put it in his barnyard where it soon learned to eat chicken feed and to behave as the chickens behaved.*

19

One day, a naturalist who was passing by inquired of the owner why an eagle, the king of all birds, should be confined to live in a barnyard with chickens. "It has never learned to fly," the farmer said.

The two men agreed to find out whether this was a permanent condition. Bently, the naturalist, took the eagle in his arms and said, "You belong in the sky and not to the earth. Stretch forth your wings and fly." The eagle was confused. He didn't know who he was. Seeing the chickens eating their food, he jumped down to be with them again.

Undismayed, the naturalist asked if he could return the next day, but the same thing happened. "May I take the eagle to the mountains?" he asked the farmer. "Sure," said the farmer, "but it will do you no good. He thinks he's a chicken."

The next day the naturalist took the eagle to a peak of the mountains nearby. He said to the eagle, "You are an eagle. Fly." Nothing. Raising the bird on his gloved arm, he shouted, "You're an eagle. Stretch forth your wings and fly."

The eagle looked around, back toward the farm where it had lived, up to the sky. Still, it did nothing. Then the naturalist pointed the bird straight at the sun. "You're an eagle, not a chicken," he shouted. The eagle began to tremble. Then he slowly stretched his wings. At last with a triumphant cry, he soared into the heavens.

— Anonymous

The gospel of John reports that Jesus said, "... No one can see the kingdom of God unless he is born again" (John 3:3). Like the eagle that thought he was a chicken, we were born to soar high and see things with an eagle's eye.

The message of the fourth gospel is "Don't despair." Despair means suffering without hope. How do we avoid despair? Trust in the Lord Jesus Christ, soar on wings like eagles and see things from a high perspective. *The Eagle* is about this message.

The apostle John, apparently the youngest of the apostles, was dear to Jesus. Along with Peter and James, John was a part of Jesus'

20

inner circle. John 13:23-25 describes John leaning on Jesus' chest at the Last Supper. John 19:25-27 says that from the cross Jesus made John a new son of his mother, clearly encouraging him to take care of Mary. John 20:2 tells us that John and Peter were the first apostles to meet Mary Magdalene as she returned from the empty tomb with the message of Jesus' resurrection. John 20:20 indicates that John was present at the appearance of risen Jesus at the Lake of Galilee where he received a message about long life. John was "the beloved disciple" who personally heard Jesus urge him and others, "Don't despair. Soar high and see things from an eternal perspective."

The higher perspective Jesus offers in this gospel is passionate, profound, and personal. This gospel is like a letter written to us by a wise, old friend. If we respond with faith, our response is gratefulness for help with the pilgrimage of faith.

While *The Eagle* is not a systematic study or a running commentary on the fourth gospel primarily for scholars and theologians, some background on the writing of the fourth gospel may be helpful. The apostle John may have had help from a scribe in writing this gospel. Knowing the other three gospels, John felt some additional parts of the story of Jesus and the meaning of what Jesus said and did needed to be shared. About the year AD 100, in his old age in Ephesus, John wrote and spoke the words we know as the fourth gospel.[1] He may have had help from a scribe who wrote some or all of the words down.[2] With an eagle's eye, the fourth gospel addresses at least three vital situations.

First, Christians were being persecuted. Some were dying for the faith. Rome had killed all the other apostles. Only John was left. The fourth gospel is a historical account and a spiritual account of the life of Jesus offering a higher perspective to address the needs of suffering Christians. John himself was later exiled to Patmos. "Don't despair," Jesus says. "I will not leave you alone" (John 14:18).

Second, Christianity had gone into the Gentile world. It was no longer made up of only Jews. When John wrote, Christianity was a mixture of Gentile and Jewish believers. Perhaps that's why John starts his gospel not with the birth of Jesus, but with "The

Word." The Greek idea of the *Logos* may have been the context for John writing about Jesus as the Word. The Greek concept of an unseen world being the real world and this world being a shadowy copy of the unseen may have been background for the fourth gospel. Thoroughly Jewish, John nevertheless takes the Greek culture into consideration.

Third, heresies abounded in the time of John. Gnostics taught that matter is evil and that God who is pure could have had nothing to do with the creation of an evil world. John writes that Jesus is the Word "through whom all things were made" (John 1:3). He adds, "God loved *the world*" (John 3:16). The gnostics held that Jesus was not really God. The fourth gospel says, "In the beginning was the Word, and the Word was with God, and the Word was God" (John 1:1). John's corrective for the Gnostic view of a totally evil world with which God could not be associated is clear: "The Word became flesh and made his dwelling among us" (John 1:14).

There are many unique features to the fourth gospel that don't appear in the synoptic gospels (Matthew, Mark, and Luke). For example, we find Jesus' long speeches, rather than parables in John's gospel. In the fourth gospel we also meet an emphasis on salvation in the here and now as well as in the afterlife. "I tell you the truth, whoever hears my word and believes him who sent me *has* eternal life" (John 5:24). In addition, Jesus' "I am" statements only appear in John's gospel.

The twelve chapters of *The Eagle* pick up on these and other unique elements of John's gospel. There is so much profound meaning in this gospel I feel like a boy standing on the shore of the ocean, trying to find a way to describe the vastness and depth of what he sees. The twelve chapters in this book by no means do justice to covering the material in this exciting and powerful gospel. I have limited myself to these twelve sections so that the length of this book will make it useable by groups for study purposes.

In addition to individuals studying *The Eagle* for personal growth, the projected audience for this book is pastors who preach and teach about this gospel. The audience is also projected to be study groups: koinonia (fellowship) or growth groups that meet in the homes of members, adult Sunday school classes, pastor's classes for new members, and people on retreats.

Questions at the end of each chapter will help all groups in their study of the material here. These questions should stimulate conversation.

There are many people who stand behind the writing of a book. Earlier I mentioned the Younker and the Franing families. Gratefulness is also expressed to the many members of the churches I have served. In Lebanon, Indiana; Muncie, Indiana; Davenport, Iowa; Tucson, Arizona; and Fountain Valley, California; many laypeople have taught me much about the Bible and living the Christian life. These faithful disciples have been instrumental in keeping my discouragement from turning into despair. These high-flying eagles have helped me gain the higher perspective of faith in Christ.

Blessings for your adventure in studying this book and the fourth gospel with an eagle's eye, looking for new ways to avoid despair and embrace the fullness of Jesus' love, light, and life. As you begin, consider the words of Martin Luther: "We propose to consider his (John's) gospel in the name of the Lord, discuss it, and preach it as long as we are able, to the glory of our Lord Christ and to our own welfare, comfort, and salvation."[3]

---

1. The unique features of John's gospel include: the marriage feast at Cana (2:1-11); the story of Nicodemus (3:1-15); the story of the Samaritan woman at the well (chapter 4); the raising of Lazarus (ch. 11); the washing of the disciples' feet (13:4-12); and Jesus' teaching about the comforter (chs. 14-17).

2. The scribe who may have done some or all of the writing of the gospel of John is called John the Elder by some scholars. John the Elder was a disciple of the apostle John. To pursue the authorship question further, see Barclay's *The Gospel Of St. John*, *The Interpreter's Bible*, William Temple's *Readings In St. John's Gospel*, or other modern commentaries on the gospel of John.

3. Martin Luther, *Luther's Works*, volume 22, *Sermons On The Gospel of St. John*, chapters 1-4, edited by Jaroslav Pelikan (St. Louis: Concordia, 1957), p. 5.

Tips For Leaders

This book is designed for group discussion as well as individual reading. If you are a discussion leader of a small group, a Bible study class, a pastor's class for new members, an adult Sunday school class, or a retreat, you may appreciate some tips on conducting your group sessions.

1. Pray in advance for the Holy Spirit to guide the group. Begin and/or end each session with prayer.

2. Use the questions at the end of each chapter to help your group discuss the material and relate it to their lives.

3. Remember, you are not a lecturer on the material. You are a discussion leader.

4. Ask questions rather than make statements. That encourages participation.

5. For best results, each group member should have a copy of *The Eagle*. Have several extra copies of the book available for new group members.

6. Each participant should read an assigned chapter of the book in advance of the session. Some will do it regularly. Others will not. Don't embarrass anyone by asking, "Who read the chapter this week?" All participants should be encouraged to discuss the topic, whether or not they have read the chapter in advance. Remember, each chapter is designed to be a springboard to discussion and relating biblical truths to life. Encourage different points of view and stories.

7. The theme running through *The Eagle* like a thread is "Don't despair." Be sure to encourage people to discuss what experiences bring us to the brink of suffering without hope and what factors keep hope alive.

8. Some chapters may require more than one session. Be flexible.

9. Some group members may talk a lot. Others may be more reserved and may need encouragement to participate.

10. For further information about group techniques and dynamics, see *Way to Grow! (Dynamic Church Growth Through Small Groups)* by Ron Lavin (available from CSS Publishing Co., 517 South Main St., Lima, Ohio 45804. Phone 800-537-1030 or email orders@csspub.com to order books).

Chapter 1

Behold The Word ... The Light ... And The Lamb

John 1:1-50

Sir James Simpson, the great scientist who contributed so much to the discovery of anesthesia, was once asked by one of his students what he considered his greatest discovery. The Scotsman replied in a voice that trembled when he spoke, "Young man, my greatest discovery is that I am a great sinner and that Jesus Christ is a great Savior."

That discovery is what chapter 1 of the gospel of John is all about. Having made that discovery, the author of the fourth gospel wants others to make it, too. He points to Jesus Christ as the Word, the light of the world, and the Lamb of God who takes away the sins of the world.

Behold The Word

"In the beginning was the Word, and the Word was with God, and the Word was God. He was with God in the beginning. Through him, all things were made; without him nothing was made that has been made" (John 1:1-3). "The Word became flesh and made his dwelling among us. We have seen his glory, the glory of the One and Only, who came from the Father, full of grace and truth" (John 1:14-15).

Martin Luther summarized the meaning of the second article of the Apostles' Creed as well as these verses about the Word of

God in the *Small Catechism*: "I believe that Jesus Christ, true God, begotten of the Father from eternity, and also true man, born of the Virgin Mary, is my Lord."[1]

That Jesus is the Word of God means that he is the true God. Jesus was not merely the best man who ever lived; he wasn't just another founder of a great world religion; he wasn't just the best example of morality or the greatest teacher of values the world has ever known. All that is true enough, but not big enough. The clear biblical witness is that Jesus Christ is God's Word made flesh.

As we shall see in greater detail in chapter 6, Jesus uses the name "I AM" for himself eight times in the gospel of John. "I AM" is God's name, according to Exodus 3:13-15. Moses asked God for his name that he might tell the people in Egypt who sent him. "Tell them I AM WHO I AM sent you," God replied. Jesus claimed the very name of God for himself. You can call him an egocentric maniac or you can accept him as God incarnate as he claims, but you cannot regulate him to *mere* humanity. Jesus was divine. Yes, but Jesus was also truly human.

That Jesus is the Word of God means that he is both divine and human. "The Word was God" (John 1:1). That Word was also human. "The Word became flesh" (John 1:14). That Jesus is human means that he completely identifies with our human situation. Bone of my bones, flesh of my flesh, blood of my blood; Jesus is my brother. As God was out in front of the Hebrews in the wilderness in the pillar of cloud by day and the pillar of fire by night, so in the person of Jesus, God goes before me in my life's journey. All suffering that I experience passes through him before it hits me. He is the suffering servant who died on the cross so that I need never feel that I am left alone. "I will not leave you as orphans," Jesus says (John 14:18). The humanity of Christ brings me hope that I will never be forsaken, because Jesus came to earth to enter all that is human, even sin. "God made him who had no sin to be sin (a sin offering) for us, so that in him we might become the righteousness of God" (2 Corinthians 5:21).

Jesus tabernacled among us. That means he pitched his tent here. If you've ever gone camping, you know what pitching your tent means. You set up temporary residence in a place different than your home. That's what "making his dwelling" (1:14b) literally means. Jesus' real home is heaven. His temporary residence was the earth. At one point in time, for about 33 years, Jesus made his temporary home with us.

The paradox of Jesus' divinity and humanity is not fully grasped by the human mind, but it is the revealed truth of scripture. That is mystery enough, but there is more to this mystery of the Word of God.

That Jesus is the Word of God also means that he is my Lord and my Savior. To be sure, he is *the* Lord and Savior. He died for all. He was crucified that all might be saved.

Jesus is the redeemer, whether we like it or not. He is Lord and Savior whether or not we accept him as such. Jesus is not sitting on Cloud 18, trembling for fear of being voted out of office. Though the world may reject him, he is nevertheless *the* Lord. The tragedy of human rejection is described in John 1:10: "He was in the world, and though the world was made through him, the world did not recognize him." He is not only the instrument of creation. He is also the redeemer who accomplished victory over sin, death, and the devil on the cross for our sakes, even when we don't recognize what he has done.

The gift of salvation has been given, but not everyone has appropriated the gift and received its benefits. It's like receiving a check for $1,000,000 with no strings attached, but unless and until you turn that check over and personally endorse it, the benefits of the gift are not yours. In like manner, until I accept Christ as *my* Lord and Savior, what he has done for me is not personally mine. Trusting him as my Lord and Savior is the way for me to appropriate what has been accomplished.

That Jesus is my Lord means that I should seek to place everything under his leadership — my home, my family, my job, my money, my interests — everything. That Jesus is *my* Savior means that I personally appropriate what he has accomplished on the cross. Salvation is to be found in this one man. There is no salvation in any other name (Acts 4:12). Through Jesus Christ, we have eternal light for our path.

Jesus is not only *a* light of salvation for the world; the fourth gospel teaches he is *the* light of salvation for the world. Boris Pasternak, the author of *Doctor Zhivago*, speaks of the uniqueness of Jesus as *the* light of salvation for the world.

> *Rome was a flea market of borrowed gods and con-*
> *quered peoples, a bargain basement on two floors, earth*
> *and heaven, a mass of filth convoluted in a triple knot*
> *as in an intestinal obstruction ... And then, into this*
> *tasteless heap of gold and marble He came, light and*
> *clothed in an aura, emphatically human, deliberately*
> *provincial, Galilean, and at that moment gods and na-*
> *tions ceased to be and man came into being....*[2]

Behold The Light

"Through him (the Word) all things were made, without him nothing was made that has been made. In him was life and that life was the light of men. The light shines in the darkness, but the darkness has not understood it" (John 1:3-5). "The true light that gives light to every man was coming into the world" (John 1:9). Jesus said, "I am the light of the world" (John 9:5).

No one but Jesus is the light of salvation. John the Baptist was not the light. He was a witness to the light (John 1:6-7). John pointed to the light that enlightens every man, woman, and child who will not resist it. Of course, many still resist letting the light shine in their darkness for fear of being exposed, but in all who receive Jesus' light, darkness is conquered.

The darkness of the world did not understand the light (John 1:5 NIV), or as other translations read: "The darkness did not overcome the light" (RSV); "... comprehend the light" (KJV); "... cannot quench it" (NEB); "... never put it out" (Phillips). Darkness doesn't win the battle with light. Light is victorious over darkness. Jesus was crucified. It looked like darkness had overcome light, but that was an illusion. Surprise — three days later, Jesus rose from the dead, showing the triumph of light over darkness. In our day, too, the apparent triumph of darkness over light is an illusion.

Sarah made this discovery as an adult. She knew something was missing in her life, but she didn't know what. Her roommate in college invited her to attend church with her. There she found what was missing. She said, "Jesus brought light to my darkness. He filled the hole in my soul." Soon after being baptized and becoming a member of a Lutheran church in Chicago, Sarah volunteered to be a Sunday school teacher. She loved children and felt that as she taught them, she, too, would learn more. After a year of teaching, Sarah was asked to lead the Sunday school Christmas play.

Leading the Christmas play with all the children was not an easy task, but Nicole, a little girl with stringy hair, dirty fingernails, and a runny nose was particularly difficult. She kept away from the other children and always had to have the last word. "God, give me strength," Sarah prayed.

When Sarah asked the children who wanted a speaking part in the play, many hands went up, but not Nicole's. When Sarah asked Nicole about it privately, the little girl, with arms folded, said, "Who said I was coming to your Christmas play?" At the dress rehearsal, Nicole muttered, "Mary doesn't look like she's gonna have a baby." The Sunday school teacher was beside herself, especially when Nicole rushed up to the crib while the children sang "Silent Night."

"Nicole, what are you doing up there?"

"Just lookin'. Besides, it's not a baby, just a doll."

The night of the play, Sarah seated Nicole right next to her. When she realized Nicole was gone, it was too late. The little girl stomped her way to the manger, just as she had done at the rehearsal. But this time, she stiffened, awestruck by what she saw. She hurried back to the pew and said in a penetrating whisper, "He's alive."

Like ripples in the crowd, the message passed from pew to pew. "He's alive. Alive. He's alive."

When the play ended, Sarah turned to Nicole and said, "I love you."

Nicole replied, "I know."

The light of God is alive today. That light penetrates the darkness and overcomes it. Jesus is the light of the world. Jesus is also the lamb of God.

Behold The Lamb

About himself, John the Baptist said, "I am not the Christ ... I am the voice of one calling in the desert, 'Make straight the way for the Lord' " (John 1:20-23). When he saw Jesus the next day, he said to two of his disciples, "Look, the Lamb of God!" (John 1:35).

Lambs were sacrificial animals in Jesus' day. They were offered on the altar to God as an appeasing sacrifice for sins. This statement by John the Baptist means at least three things.

First, it means that forgiveness comes from the Lord Jesus Christ. The Baptist verbalized what Christians have repeated ever since: Animal sacrifices are no longer necessary since on the cross Jesus made the sacrifice for sins that makes it possible for all who confess their sins to be forgiven. The sacrifice of Christ as the Lamb of God is foreshadowed by the offering of a lamb by Abraham instead of his son, Isaac (Genesis 22:8), predicted by the prophet Isaiah (Isaiah 53:7), and described in Revelation 5:9 — "You are worthy to take the scroll and open its seals, because you were slain, and with your blood you purchased men for God from every tribe and language and people and nation."

The apostle John, the author of the book of Revelation,[3] adds, "Worthy is the Lamb, who was slain, to receive power and wealth and wisdom and strength and honor and glory and praise!" (Revelation 5:12).

The Lamb of God is worthy of our praise because he makes the forgiveness of sins possible. He paid the price of sin — suffering and death. The sins of us all were laid on his back the Friday we call "Good." He became sin that we might be forgiven of sin.

Second, the statement of Baptist demonstrates humility before the almighty. "He [Jesus] is the Lamb of God, not me," John is saying. "I baptize with water, but among you stands one you do not know. He is the one who comes after me, the thongs of whose sandals I am not worthy to untie" (John 1:26-27). "He must become greater; I must become less," he added later (John 3:30). The Baptist is humbled in the presence of his cousin, Jesus.

We cannot be humble by our own efforts. We are humbled by the greatness of something or someone so superior to us that we realize just how small we are. If you have ever stood at the bottom of the Grand Canyon and looked up, you had a sense of how small you are by comparison. Humility is not a matter of crunching down and pretending to be less than we are. It's a matter of stretching out to our full height, but looking at that which dwarfs us by comparison. The Baptist's statements show that's what happened to him when he said, "Behold the Lamb of God."

Third, the statement, "Look, the Lamb of God!" sets an example for witnessing. Witnessing for Christ means testifying to what you have seen, heard, and experienced. We pick up the story of Jesus and John the Baptist in verse 32 of chapter 1. "Then John gave his testimony: 'I saw the Spirit come down from heaven as a dove and remain on him....' " That's witnessing.

When two of John's disciples heard him speaking about Jesus as the Lamb of God, they followed where Jesus went. One of those disciples was Andrew who found his brother, Peter, and told him, "We have found the Messiah" (John 1:41). That's witnessing.

Philip, who heard all this, found Nathaniel and told him, "We have found the one Moses wrote about in the Law, and about whom the prophets also wrote — Jesus of Nazareth, the son of Joseph" (John 1:44-45). That's witnessing, too.

Witnessing means telling the truth about what you have seen. Jesus told the apostles (and us through them), "... You will be my witness in Jerusalem, and in all Judea and Samaria, and to the ends of the earth" (Acts 1:8). That's quite a commission! The reason for all this witnessing is that Christians are called to help people make the greatest discovery in the world: that they are sinners and that Jesus is a great Savior.

A psychiatrist came to my office to see me one day. "My life is falling apart," he said, "I have been attending worship and listening to your sermons for several weeks now. Each week I slipped out the door during the last hymn so that you would not see me. After listening to your sermons, I think I can trust you. I have serious family problems. I don't believe in my work anymore. I'm depressed." Then he paused and added, "I'm a Christian. I follow Christian principles."

"Did you ever stop to think that being a Christian is more than following Christian principles?" I asked. "Being a Christian is a matter of following Christ."

"Oh," he said. "I hadn't stopped to think of it that way."

Thus began a spiritual awakening and a friendship that within a year produced a book the psychiatrist and I coauthored. The book title was *Jesus Christ, The Liberator.*[4]

Jesus Christ, the liberator, is the Word of God, the light of the world, and the Lamb of God who takes away the sins of the world. That is the greatest discovery a person can make.

---

1. Martin Luther, *The Small Catechism* (Minneapolis: Augsburg Fortress, 1979), p. 13.

2. Boris Pasternak, *Doctor Zhivago* (New York: Pantheon Books, Inc., 1948), p. 43.

3. The apostle John, or his scribe(s) wrote Revelation, 1 John, 2 John, and 3 John, as well as the gospel of John.

4. Ron Lavin and Bill Grimmer, M.D., *Jesus Christ, The Liberator* (Lima, Ohio: CSS Publishing Company, Inc., 1974).

Questions For Your Personal Consideration And/Or Group Discussion

1. When you were a child, how did you picture Jesus?

2. To speak of Jesus as God's Word became flesh means _____
    _____
    _____

3. What is the difference between saying, "Jesus is *the* Lord" and saying, "Jesus is *my* Lord"?

4. Have you ever been trapped in darkness? What difference did light make?

5. That Jesus is the Lamb of God means _____
    _____
    _____

6. Read and discuss Isaiah 53:7.

7. Read and discuss Revelation 5:12.

8. Discuss the following statement: "Humility is not a matter of crunching down and pretending to be less than you are, but stretching out to our full height before that which dwarfs us by comparison."

9. Think of yourself walking along the wind-swept shore of a great ocean. The waves are roaring. It is late at night and there are no people around. The moonbeams are dancing on the top of the waves, like so many children at play. Think about the ocean. It stretches out before you, far beyond the vision of your eyes. You know only a little bit of the shallow waters of the shoreline. There are mysteries unknown and depths that have never been discovered. In what ways is this like saying, "Jesus is my Lord and Savior"?

10. How does this chapter connect with the theme "Don't despair"?

Chapter 2

Will You Come To The Party?

John 2:1-11

In chapter 1 of the gospel of John, we encountered Jesus saying to two of the disciples of John the Baptist, who asked where he was going, "Come and you will see" (John 1:19). Andrew, one of the two disciples, was so taken with what he saw and heard that he extended the invitation to his brother, Peter. "We have found the Messiah," he said (John 1:41). Philip, a friend of Andrew and Peter, found Nathaniel and told him, "We have found the one Moses wrote about in the Law and about whom the prophets also wrote — Jesus of Nazareth, the son of Joseph" (John 1:45).

These invitations were to come to a celebration of an enlargement of life. That's what's missing in many of our churches. Instead of inviting people to a celebration of life that fulfills our innermost longings, few Christians invite others to worship at their church, much less to the party called the kingdom of God. If they invite anyone to come to church, the tendency is to imply duty or responsibility or even worse, to invite others to come because we need help in supporting the church budget or making building fund pledges. No wonder unchurched people think about the church as an institution filled with lots of hypocrites.

When Jesus said, "You will be my witnesses" (Acts 1:8), he didn't have the institutional church in mind. He was thinking of the church as a vital, dynamic community more like a party than a congregational meeting. The church is an institution, but that's secondary. Primarily, the church is "the communion of saints"

37

(Apostles' Creed, Article Three). In that communion of forgiven sinners, there is joy and celebration.

Here in chapter 2 of the fourth gospel, we have the wonderful biblical corrective of how people think about Christianity and church. Here we meet the good news head on: The kingdom of God is a party. Christians can invite outsiders to a wonderful party. Non-Christians can have their preconceptions about God and his church popped like so many balloons if they pay attention to what Jesus teaches about what it means to follow him. It's like coming to a wedding reception where people are having fun.

At a recent wedding reception, I talked with one of the bridesmaids. After some informal conversation about the wedding, I asked about her and her church.

"I don't have a church," she said. "I don't worship anywhere anymore. I used to go, but there were too many rules and regulations for me. Don't get me wrong, I still pray sometimes." Then she paused thoughtfully and said, "I guess you could call me a Light Baptist."

There are some Light Lutherans, too, I thought. "You mean like Bud Light," I said, looking at the beer in her hand.

"Something like that," she said. "I still believe that there is a God, and we can call on him when we really need him, but this church stuff turns me off. I'm not a card-carrying Christian."

I did the best I could do to encourage her to think of the church in a different way — as a place of joy and celebration. Then I gave her my business card. "The Bible teaches that Christianity is like a party. If you ever want to talk about that and consider the church as a place of joy and happiness, give me a ring and we can get together." Then, with a smile on my face, I added, "You need never again say you are not a "card-carrying Christian.' " She smiled back, but she never called.

It's bad enough that people think of the church only in terms of rules, regulations, and responsibilities. It's sadder still when people think of God that way.

At another wedding reception, a man answered my question about his church and faith by saying, "I don't believe in God."

"Tell me about the god you don't believe in," I replied. "Chances are I don't believe in that god, either."

"What do you mean?" he stammered.

"The god most people say they don't believe in is the god that runs down little children with Mack trucks or starts wars or doesn't care when innocent people suffer. That's not the God and Father of our Lord Jesus Christ. I don't believe in that god, either. If you want to talk further about that, give me a ring," I said, handing him my business card.

He phoned. We talked about the illusions people have about God and his church. We talked about the kingdom of God as a party with God as the host. Eventually, this man started to attend worship. He also attended a pastor's class. On the day John and his children were baptized, a great party was held. His wife was ecstatic. "How'd you do it?" she asked. "John has been a stubborn unbeliever all the time I've known him. Now, suddenly, he's an enthusiastic Christian."

"I didn't do it," I said. "The Holy Spirit just freed John from some of the illusions he had about God and his church."

That's why John 2:1-11 is so important. At the wedding reception party in Cana of Galilee, Jesus brought a bright light to the dull, dark way people think about church and God. He took ordinary water and made something extraordinary out of it. The wine is a sign of what the kingdom of God is like.

Of course, the kingdom of God is not the church, but the church should reflect the values of the kingdom. The kingdom of God will only come at the end of time when Jesus comes to judge the living and the dead and Jesus reigns as Lord of all. In this life, we have previews of coming attractions. Churches should offer those previews. Here we have only intimations of what awaits us in heaven, but Christians and local congregations should be reflecting the qualities of that heavenly fulfillment. Local congregations should be outposts of heaven. The hereafter can be reflected in the here and now. Turning water into wine is a sign of what Jesus does today in mission-minded churches. He takes the ordinary and turns it into something extraordinary. People can be transformed today.

When the master of the banquet tasted the water that Jesus turned into wine, he said, "Everyone brings out the choice wine first and then the cheaper wine after the guests have had too much to drink; but you have saved the best till now" (John 2:10). This was Jesus' first miraculous sign, John tells us (John 2:11). As the water turned into wine, so ordinary people can become extraordinary Christians!

The apostles were all ordinary people. Many of them were fishermen who looked like anything but world-changers. Yet, here we are 2,000 years later calling them Saint Peter, Saint James, and Saint John, believing in the "one, holy and apostolic church" (Nicene Creed). Amazing, isn't it? All of these apostles were persecuted, many imprisoned. All but John were martyred. John was exiled to the Island of Patmos to try to stop all this talk about Jesus and the kingdom of God. All the efforts of the Roman empire to "shut up these Christians" failed. The Roman empire is gone. Christianity lives on.

Jesus took ordinary people and turned them into extraordinary Christians. They came to the party called the kingdom of God and there found "an inexpressible and glorious joy" (1 Peter 1:8) that no human could give or take away.

Jesus is doing the same kind of thing in people's lives today. We can't make ourselves extraordinary. It is not a matter of achieving, but receiving. It is happening today, just like it did with Peter, James, and John. If people will just come to the party, they will discover what God has in store for them.

One of my favorite pictures is called *Jesus Christ, The Liberator*. It shows Jesus with his head back and his eyes sparkling, having a good time. The laughter is a symbol of what Jesus does for people. He frees people from the bondage of sin, death, and the devil. He brings fulfillment. I was not Ron Lavin until Jesus turned me from self-centeredness and selfishness to a new way of thinking. Before I came to the party, I was "Almost Ron Lavin." Afterward, I got a preview of what I was intended to be. Even when we slip and sin, we can remember the signs of liberation and joy given to us by God.

The Bible teaches that Christians are both saints and sinners. That means even when we are turned from self-centeredness and selfishness, we still return to old patterns and old ways, but we can always remember the taste of the new wine at Jesus' party. The wine of holy communion is a frequent reminder of what God has done and is doing in our lives.

Another of my favorite pictures of Jesus is called *The Risen Christ By The Sea*. In this picture, Jesus is holding a net and over his shoulder is pictured a fishing boat. The picture says, "Go and fish for people and share the joy you have found in me." I first discovered this picture when I became a member of the Fellowship of Merry Christians and started to receive their *Joyful Noiseletter*.[1]

Merry Christians give generously and cheerfully because they know "God loves a cheerful giver" (2 Corinthians 9:7). That's much better than giving grudgingly.

Merry Christians naturally share the good news of Christ with others. Merry Christians invite people to come to the party called the kingdom of God. At this party, we have our vertical relationship with God restored through Jesus Christ. We also discover a new dimension of joy in our brothers and sisters.

Merry Christians share a special fellowship called koinonia. Koinonia is fellowship, in depth, in Christ, for mission. In small groups, Christians grow in understanding and perspective.[2] Thus people can learn not to take themselves too seriously.

As Victor Borge, the comedian, said, "Laughter is the shortest distance between people." Merry Christians, with perspective from God and in fellowship with one another, know that. It's no wonder that people come to the party when joyful, merry Christians invite them.

---

1. If you are interested in a more joyful life, consider joining the Fellowship of Merry Christians and getting their monthly newsletter, *The Joyful Noiseletter*, write to them at P. O. Box 895, Portage, Michigan 49081-0895; phone: 1-800-877-2757; email: JoyfulNA@aol.com; web site: www.joyfulnewsletter.com.

2. Ron Lavin, *Way To Grow! (Dynamic Church Growth Through Small Groups)* (Lima, Ohio: CSS Publishing Company, Inc., 1996).

Questions For Your Personal Consideration
And/Or Group Discussion

1. If you are in a group, share some joyful experience you have had. What happens when you share this kind of experience?

2. A three-step spiritual exercise.

   a. Think about some person who showed you love. Perhaps it was when you were small. Perhaps it happened more recently. Now put that person's name in the following sentence, adding the way in which they made you feel loved. "_____ loved me by _____."
   In my case, I put, "Walter loved me when I was fifteen by telling me that he believed in me." Walter was the foreman at a tool and die shop in Chicago. At the time, I worked part-time for that tool and die shop. When Walter took me aside and told me he had been watching my work and liked what he saw, I was on cloud nine. When he added, "I believe in you, Ron," that made an unforgettable impression on my mind. Later when I became a Christian, I was able to look back on that statement and see that God used it as a seed, which would later blossom.

   b. Next, substitute the name Christ for the name you put in the sentence. In my case, the sentence now reads: "Christ loved me by believing in me."

   c. This week, commit yourself to doing for someone else what has been done for you. I my case, I will tell someone that I believe in them.

3. If you are in a small group or adult education class, the next time you meet, share what happened when you showed love for someone else the way you had experienced it. The principle behind this witnessing exercise is that we can witness to others about what we have experienced. We can help other

people feel loved, even as we have felt loved. This is an important step in inviting people to the fulfillment in Christ they were intended to experience when they were born.

4. Reread John 2:4-6. What's going on between Mary and Jesus? As you answer this question, consider two things:

   a. "Woman" in the original Greek text is *gunai*. In English, the term seems rough, abrupt, and discourteous. In fact, *gunai* is a term of respect. Jesus uses it again from the cross when he tells his mother to take care of the apostle John and John to take care of her (John 19:26).

   b. When we consider the meaning of the term *gunai* and then note Mary's reaction, we see that Jesus apparently spoke to his mother at the wedding banquet in a gentle rather than a harsh way. He seems to be saying, "Don't worry. I will take care of this matter my way at the appropriate time."

Chapter 3

How Can A Person Be Born Again?

John 3:1-36

The third chapter of John is like a many-sided diamond. Each side sparkles as the light shines on it. As we consider the question, "How can a person be born again?" we will look at three of the gem-like sides of this text: 1) water and the Spirit (3:1-13), 2) the cross of Christ (3:14-15), and 3) the love of God (3:16-21).

The chapter opens with Nicodemus, a wealthy Pharisee and member of the Jewish supreme court, coming to Jesus by night. Coming by night may be a sign of Nicodemus' cautious nature or merely a way to get away from the crowds that surrounded Jesus during the day. Maybe Nicodemus did not want anyone to see him seeking Jesus. After all, he was a teacher of the law and a member of the Sanhedrin. An additional reason for the nocturnal visit may have been that the Jewish rabbis had a saying, "Night is the best time to study the law."

Whatever the reason for the coming by night, Nicodemus wanted to talk about religion. "Rabbi," he began, "we know you are a teacher who has come from God. For no one could perform the miraculous signs you are doing if God were not with him" (John 3:2). Jesus quickly moved from talking about religion to talking personally to Nicodemus in a way that shook his foundations.

"No one can see the kingdom of God unless he is born again," Jesus said. He cut right to the heart of the matter. He got beyond the facade of talking about theology and told Nicodemus what must happen to him if he was to be a part of the kingdom.

"How can a man be born when he is old?" Nicodemus replied. Jesus explained that he was talking about spiritual, not physical, rebirth.

Born Again Of Water And The Spirit

In the late-night dialogue, Jesus went right to the root of the matter. "I tell you the truth, no one can enter the kingdom of God unless he is born of water and the Spirit" (John 3:3). Nicodemus, a proud and respected Pharisee, was shaken by this pointed, personal remark about rebirth by water and the Spirit. Jesus intended that. Sometimes we have to be shaken to the roots of our being before we give our attention to what God wants to do for us.

A story is told about Grandpa, who went to see the dentist because he had a terrible toothache. "Open up," said the dentist. "Let me have a look." Grandpa shook his head. "If you don't open up, I can't work on your tooth," the dentist replied. No response. "Come back tomorrow," the dentist said. The next day, the same thing happened. Grandpa was afraid. "Come back tomorrow," the dentist said.

"If this happens again tomorrow," the dentist told his assistant, "stick this pin into his bottom. He'll open his mouth and I can pull his tooth." The next day when the old man refused to open his mouth, the dentist winked at the assistant who promptly stuck a pin in Grandpa's behind. The dentist reached into Grandpa's mouth and pulled the tooth. When it was all over, the dentist said, "Now that wasn't so bad, was it?"

"No," said Grandpa, "but those roots sure go deep."

Our stubborn resistance to God's way of doing things is something like that. We want our pain to stop, but we refuse to "open up" to God. He goes to the root of the matter and tells us that nothing less than rebirth is necessary for us to get right with him and become part of the kingdom of God.

The kingdom of God is God's rule over us for our own good. Nicodemus had religion. He needed rebirth and submission to Jesus as Lord. A little religion doesn't give us enough power to punch our way out of a paper bag. But submission to Jesus as Lord gives us an unconquerable partnership in this life with eternal results in the next life. That's what spiritual rebirth into the kingdom of God is all about.

God's kingdom doesn't come in its fullness until the end of time. When Jesus returns in glory to judge the living and the dead, we will fully experience his kingdom rule and all that it means. The kingdom of God is a future reality, but it is also a present reality. In the hereafter, Jesus will reign as Lord of all. In the here and now we get previews of this lordship and its wonderful consequences. In the present, we get a foretaste of the heavenly things that eye has not seen, ear has not heard, and mind has not comprehended.

The confused Nicodemus represents us all when he replies, "How can this happen?" This may be a wonderful thing, but "What must I do to be born again?"

Jesus tells him that spiritual rebirth comes through water and the Spirit.

We are spiritually reborn through water. Baptism[1] is the holy sacrament of God's action to adopt us as his children. A sacrament is a sacred act of God for forgiveness, containing an outward element and the Word of God. The outward element in Baptism is water.

Water is used in Baptism as a sign of the inner cleansing God is accomplishing. How can water do all this? Luther explains that it is not water alone, which accomplishes spiritual cleansing. "It is not water that does these things, but God's word with the water and our trust in his word. Water by itself is only water, but with the word of God it is a life-giving water which by grace gives the new birth through the Holy Spirit."[2]

The child (or adult) being baptized once and for all leaves the state of not knowing God. Baptism is the beginning of the process of rebirth, which needs to go on throughout life. Being baptized doesn't mean that the baptized person will necessarily go to heaven. Baptism is like the seed being planted. Not every planted seed blossoms. Nurture is needed for a seed to grow to fullness and harvest. For physical seeds, that nurture is with sunlight and water. For spiritual growth, nurture means education and loving examples in home and church.

Before proceeding further, we should make a clear distinction between the sacrament of Baptism and the baptism of John the Baptist. John himself made that distinction. He said, "Look, the lamb of God who takes away the sin of the world! ... I came baptizing with water ... he will baptize with the Holy Spirit" (John 1:29-34).

Acts 19:1-7 makes that same distinction. The situation is twelve men in Ephesus who had not received the Holy Spirit. "We have not even heard that there is a Holy Spirit," they said. Paul asked, "Then what baptism did you receive?"

"John's baptism," they replied.

Paul then explained, "John's baptism was a baptism of repentance. He told the people to believe in the one coming after him, that is, in Jesus." On hearing this, they were baptized into the name of the Lord Jesus.

We are reborn spiritually by the Holy Spirit. The prime purpose of the Holy Spirit is to awaken in us faith in Jesus. We receive, we don't achieve, the status of God's kingdom people. We are saved by grace, through faith, and that not of ourselves, lest anyone should boast (Ephesians 2:8). Martin Luther puts it this way:

> *I cannot by my own understanding or effort believe in the Lord Jesus Christ my Lord or come to him. But the Holy Spirit has called me through the Gospel, enlightened me with his gifts, and sanctified and kept me in true faith.*[3]

Rebirth by the Holy Spirit comes in Baptism. It also comes in other ways. As Luther points out, "We must renew our Baptism daily by repentance." For some, repentance comes when they find themselves in suffering. Repentance is turning back to God by submission to the lordship of Christ. For some it comes only when they are wiped out like a dish as to their own strength.

For others, the awakening by the Holy Spirit, comes from seeing the suffering of others or seeing and hearing their witness. One of my confirmation students was awakened when she went to Bethphage Mission in Axtel, Nebraska, where mentally and physically handicapped people are cared for in loving ways. Here's what happened as described in a letter she wrote to me.

Recently, I began to think of how I felt three or four years ago. When I was in my junior high years, I honestly thought I was a woman of the world. I thought I knew so much I didn't need help from anyone. The thought of needing to be born again never crossed my mind. I was a little shaky inside because I felt somewhat threatened and unsure, but never admitted it.

In confirmation class, I began to question my former false confidence, but I never did anything about it. Pastor, you gave me the confirmation Bible verse, "Be still and know I am God" (Psalm 46:10), but I didn't understand it then.

Bethphage changed all that. Originally I went thinking, "I'll go and get my dad 'off my back' by doing something he approves of for a change." I also thought that it might be good to do something nice for some needy people.

Once I got there, it hit me. Christ is in each of these people. I realized these people who love God so much had so much to teach me. Bethphage took away all my shields and false confidences. I stood stripped as to my own strengths. I felt so much guilt about my former attitude. God was waiting. I realized I could be still before him and he would take away all my sins. I felt joy, real joy.

Since then my life has been a series of ups and downs. My newfound faith has many challenges. I guess my rebirth is going to be a never-ending process and will have to be renewed throughout my life.

Born Again By The Cross Of Christ

John 3:13-15 reports that Jesus said to Nicodemus, "No one has ever gone into heaven except the one who came from heaven — the Son of Man. Just as Moses lifted up the snake in the desert, so the Son of Man must be lifted up, that everyone who believes in him may have eternal life."

The cross of Christ makes rebirth possible. Jesus took our sins upon himself that first Good Friday. Think of yourself standing at the foot of the cross, looking up into those all-knowing eyes. Look at the crown of thorns on his head. Look at the nails in his hands and feet. Hear Jesus say, "I'd rather die than let you go." Those who look up at him and accept what he did find a new life.

The gospel of John compares that sight with the sight of Moses holding up the snake on a bronze pole in the wilderness (Numbers 21:4-9). On their journey through the wilderness, the Hebrews murmured, complained, and rebelled against Moses and God. To punish them God sent deadly fiery serpents into their midst. Moses, instructed by God, held up a bronze serpent on a pole. Those Israelites who looked up at the serpent on the pole, remembered God and his power. They were healed. To this day, the symbol of the healing arts is a snake on a pole.

Jesus on the cross brings healing to our lives. No words can describe the event perfectly. All illustrations fail to fully capture all that God has done through the crucifixion. The bronze serpent story reminds us who is behind all this.

Isaiah 53 gets us in touch with the agony of it all.

"He was despised and rejected by men, a man of sorrows, and familiar with suffering. Like one from whom men hide their faces he was despised, and we esteemed him not" (Isaiah 53:3). Feel the pain in the suffering servant. Feel the willingness of him who gave up his life that we might have life.

"... He was pierced for our transgressions, he was crushed for our iniquities; the punishment that brought us peace was upon him, and by his wounds we are healed" (Isaiah 53:5). Think about the verbs that described the crucified one: pierced and crushed. Jesus' side was pierced by the soldier to make sure he was dead. The very life was crushed out of him by a process like drowning as his lungs were crushed by the pressure of shifting from the hands to the feet in agony. Albert Schweitzer described the agony of Jesus' death this way: "Jesus himself still hangs on Golgotha, a mangled corpse caught in the spokes of the world's wheel, which he has brought to a stop."[4] The focus on Jesus' agony helps us as despair moves in like a fog.

"We all, like sheep, have gone astray, each of us has turned to his own way; and the Lord has laid on him the iniquity of us all" (Isaiah 53:6). That means that at one point in time the punishment for all of the selfish acts and thoughts of all human beings was laid on one man's back. Unimaginable! Incomprehensible! Yet true!

"He was oppressed and afflicted, yet he did not open his mouth; he was led like a lamb to the slaughter, and as a sheep before her shearers is silent, so he did not open his mouth" (Isaiah 53:7). To be oppressed and afflicted means to feel the pressure from every side with no view to escape, yet Jesus was silent for long stretches of time before Pilate and Herod. He was spit upon. A crown of thorns was put on his head in mockery. He was beaten. Think of all that was done for you, in order that you might be reborn. That focus helps us be renewed when we suffer and begin to lose hope.

"For he bore the sin of many, and made intercession for the transgressors" (Isaiah 53:12). Listen as you look up into the face of Jesus. "Father forgive them. They don't know what they are doing." Think again about your own suffering by looking at Jesus' suffering. What gets your attention gets you. Give your attention to the cross.

In my many years of ministry, I have struggled to find helpful ways to get people in touch with how much Jesus has done for us. When I took confirmation students on retreat I had them stretch out their arms and put their feet together as if they were being crucified. I had them hold that position for just a few minutes so that they were feeling the pain in their arms and legs. Then we talked about all that Jesus had done to make their spiritual rebirth possible. Some of them seemed to have a better appreciation for the cross after the retreat. Some got an eagle's eye view of Jesus' suffering.

On retreat, I also used a story of a man shooting an arrow of justice at another man found guilty of a serious crime. We enacted that story. One student was selected to be the guilty criminal. Others stood on the sidelines and cheered as the pretend arrow of justice was shot at the guilty one. Then the one who shot the arrow ran out in front of it and received what had been shot and died in place of the one who should have received the deadly instrument of death. When I asked the one who was saved, how he felt when his Savior stepped in the way and died in his place, he or she usually said something like, "Amazed, relieved, grateful." But I always thought, "I wonder if any of these teenagers really got the meaning?"

The illustration of the arrow of justice is far from perfect, but one young man took the story to heart. Let's call him Charlie. Charlie was not one of my better students. At times, I wondered if he would ever get through confirmation class. Once I left the church where Charlie and his family were members, I lost track of him. One day, twenty years later, I got a letter from him saying that the story of the arrow and the guilty sinner changed his life." I've never forgotten it," he said. "It changed my life. It showed me how much God loved me." The letter was signed, "The Reverend Charles Miller."

Born Again Through The Love Of God

The most famous passage in the gospel of John, and some say the most famous passage in the Bible, is John 3:16. Nicodemus was the first one to hear the incomparable words of Jesus, "For God so loved the world that he gave his one and only Son, that whoever believes in him shall not perish but have eternal life."

Jesus had told Nicodemus that he must be born again of water and the Spirit. He had added that he would be lifted up on the cross to give rebirth to all who would look there and believe what he was doing for them. In John 3:16, Jesus tells us the motivation of God for all he does for us.

The key word in the passage is *agape*. That Greek word is one of three used in the New Testament, which we translate "love." *Eros* means selfish, "give-me" love. From this word we get the concept of erotic. *Filios* means friendship, or mutual love. *Agape* means selfless love for one's enemies. "While we were sinners Christ died for us," Saint Paul wrote. God has *agape* love for the whole world.

Note that the passage doesn't say, "God so loved the church ..." but "God so loved the world." That means that all people of every color and kind, in every land — near and far — are objects of God's self-giving love.

Pastors and teachers try to use a variety of illustrations of the meaning of the cross of Christ and the love of God for our lives

52

today. What works for one person may not work for others. Consider the parable of Goodly Almighty.

In a distant land across the ocean, there lived an elderly man named Goodly Almighty. It was not until many years after Goodly and his wife had been married that their heart's desire was met in the birth of a baby boy. The whole village rejoiced with them at the birth of the child. He was an ideal son. Goodly could not have asked for any better.

A mighty river flowed past the village where Goodly Almighty and his family lived. Barges and ships would regularly travel up and down the river transporting goods throughout the land. Going over the waters was a railroad bridge that was regularly traveled by trains. The passenger trains carried all sorts of people back and forth across the country. Rich and poor traveled together going to their various destinations. Goodly's job was to operate the railroad bridge. He turned it one way to let boats go through and another way to let trains go across.

Goodly knew the schedules perfectly, so he would always have the bridge in the right position at the right time. It meant careful timing, but in his twenty years on the job not a single mistake had been made and there were no accidents.

Goodly decided to give his young boy, Innocent, a special treat on his sixth birthday. Innocent would get to be with his dad as he worked the bridge that day.

Innocent had a wonderful time playing around the bridge and watching his dad work the levers. Goodly enjoyed having his son with him and thought about the day when Innocent would take over his job of running the bridge.

Three o'clock was a very crucial time in the day's schedule. A large southbound barge went by at that time. Immediately after it passed, the bridge would have to be turned to allow it to be in place for the 3:15 cross country train. There could be no delays. A slip up would result in the loss of hundreds of lives.

As the three o'clock barge was going by, Goodly was thinking about what a good birthday treat this day had been for his son. The barge passed and now it was time to push the red lever to bring the bridge back into place so the fast approaching train could make a safe crossing.

Suddenly, Goodly noticed that Innocent was not at his side. He had gone below the control tower to look at the gears and motor mechanism which powered the bridge. Innocent's feet were caught in the gears. He was screaming for his daddy to help him and trying desperately to pull his feet out. It was no use. He couldn't free himself.

It would take Goodly half an hour to reach his son and free him. Goodly looked up and glanced at the fast approaching train, full of people. It was right on schedule. He glanced down at his still-stuck boy.

He closed his eyes as he pushed the red lever which turned the bridge. The gears steadily pulled Innocent into the machinery and crushed the life out of him. From the control tower Goodly could hear his screams. Finally, they died out.

As the train rushed by, Goodly opened his eyes to see the people he loved. They were laughing and having a good time. Some smiled and waved at him. None of them knew the grief on the father's heart who had sacrificed his only son to a horrible death so that others might live.

— Anonymous

"God so loved the world that he gave his one and only Son that whoever believes in him shall not perish but have eternal life" (John 3:16). Out of love for us, God sacrificed his Son on the cross to give us the opportunity for new birth.

The story of Goodly Almighty was rejected by one pastor at a pastors' conference where I spoke. He said it was too simplistic. Other pastors at the same conference asked for copies because they wanted to use the story in their sermons. Many laypeople who heard this story have told me it was an eye-opener for them. No stories or

54

illustrations are perfect examples of the love of God. Different stories and illustrations about the love of God reach different people in different ways.

In this chapter, we have looked at three ways in which the third chapter of the gospel of John explains how we are born again: 1) by water and the Spirit, 2) by the cross of Christ, and 3) by the love of God. As I indicated in the beginning of this chapter, the third chapter of the fourth gospel is like a many-sided diamond. As the light shines on one side and then the next, we see different sides of the glory of God. Other magnificent sides of this many-sided gem have not even been mentioned:

- miraculous signs (3:2);
- the Spirit and the wind (3:6-8);
- heaven (3:13);
- Moses (3:14); and
- the bride and the bridegroom (3:29).

John 3:1-36 is a precious many-sided diamond. Every verse seems to be saying, "Don't despair, whatever happens to you. I love you so much that I'd rather die for you than give you up."

---

1. In this book, when the sacrament of Baptism is described, the word "Baptism" is capitalized to distinguish it from the baptism of John the Baptist and other baptisms that are in the lower case.

2. Martin Luther, *The Small Catechism* (Minneapolis: Augsburg Fortress, 1979), p. 24.

3. *Ibid*, p. 14.

4. Albert Schweitzer, as quoted by Helmut Thielicke, *Man in God's World,* tr. by John Doberstein (New York: Harper and Row, 1967), p. 122.

Questions For Your Personal Consideration And/Or Group Discussion

1. If anyone in the class or group has on a diamond ring, shine a bright light on it. A flashlight will do. In what ways is the third chapter of John like that many-sided diamond?

2. Discuss this quote from Martin Luther (*Luther's Works*, pp. 276-277):

    > *Nicodemus lived a holy and honorable life in the world and gave due attention to good works. He was a pious and influential layman and a member of the powerful Jewish court called the Sanhedrin. John says that he was one of the aristocracy, a ruler in the civil government. He comes to Christ with an irreproachable character, with decency, honorableness, and obedience to the civil office. Yet, how does the Lord receive him? He surely lays him low at first, for his hope and good opinion of himself must be crushed and must vanish. In effect, he says, "My dear Nicodemus, since you regard me as a prophet of the truth come from God, I shall tell you the truth. I shall carry out that office and inform you of the truth."*

3. When fundamentalists ask, "Have you been born again?" what do they mean? How is this different from how this chapter approaches the subject?

4. What is the difference between the baptism of John and the Baptism of Jesus?

5. What does it mean to speak of the kingdom of God as both future and present reality?

6. How would you explain spiritual rebirth to a group of teenagers?

7. Have the class or group leader read aloud the story of Goodly Almighty in this chapter. What insights into the love of God do you find here?

Chapter 4

The Shady Lady From Samaria

John 4:5-42

This story is one of the best of all biblical stories about the journey of faith from curiosity to commitment to community. We see this journey in both the shady Samaritan lady who talked to Jesus at the well and the townspeople who come out to meet the man she reports "knows everything about me."

In addition, this is a great story because it contains the power to re-awaken spiritually insensitive people like the Samaritans. The Samaritans had drifted into the worship of false gods and immorality. The Samaritan race had emerged when the Jews in Judah were conquered by Nebuchadnezzar, the Babylonian king. He deported them to Babylon (today's Iraq) in 586 BC. The remaining Jews had intermarried with pagans and fallen away from the worship of the one true God and from ethical behavior. They forgot the main tenets of Judaism — monotheism and morality.

The Jews of Jesus' time, living in the northern kingdom of Israel and the southern kingdom of Judah, hated the Samaritans. They wouldn't even go into Samaria. They walked far out of their way, around Samaria, to get to the northern or southern kingdoms. Jesus went into Samaria, the territory of the people who forgot who they were.

In our day, spiritually sleepy people fall into the worship of false gods, who are not God, in a wide variety of ways — worshiping the god of pleasure, the god of materialism, the god of humanism, the god of the New Age Movement, the god of ethical relativism, or the gods of the hundreds of other religions that have emerged in our time. Many have drifted away from what they were taught as children about God and Jesus as children. Many have forgotten the fundamental's morality — the difference between good and evil — and fallen into the trap of ethical relativism. This story is an encouragement to return to the truth about God and Christian behavior as Christians have taught it for over 2,000 years and to discover it as a new reality.

T. S. Eliot wrote:

> *The end of all our exploring will be*
> *to arrive where we started*
> *and know the place for the first time.*[1]

That's what is happening in the story of the shady lady from Samaria — the return to where we started, but forgot, and the discovery of it for the first time. As Brennan Manning puts it, "We often forget to remember who we are." As we look more closely at the journey from curiosity to commitment to community, we may discover who we are in the story.

A Wonder Bread® commercial from some years ago describes its product like this: "Taste it again for the first time." Our spiritual journey back to the one true God and his ways through Jesus Christ amounts to the same kind of experience. Many have come to think of Christianity as something that is dull, drab, and dysfunctional for modern men and women. "Taste it again for the first time," and you will see just how wrong that is. Move with the people in our story from curiosity to commitment to community.

Curiosity
The Samaritan woman is drawn into a relationship with Christ out of curiosity. She is surprised he is willing to talk with her at all because he is a Jew and the Jews of her time hate the Samaritans for compromising their heritage. Her curiosity is stirred to a fever pitch by Jesus' willingness to talk to her. In Jesus' time, the Jews taught that only men should talk about the law, theology,

and matters related to God. Jesus talks about religion to a Samaritan woman — a scandal of the first magnitude.

The Samaritan woman is deeply moved by the way Jesus talks to her near Jacob's well. "Will you give me a drink?" he asks politely.

"You are a Jew and I am a Samaritan woman. How can you ask me for a drink?"

She is stunned when he replies, "If you knew the gift of God and who it is that asks you for a drink, you would have asked him and he would have given you living water ... Everyone who drinks of this water will be thirsty again, but whoever drinks the water I give him will never thirst. Indeed, the water I give him will become in him a spring of water welling up to eternal life."

Notice the major shift, a dramatic reversal, in topics from water to the water of eternal life. This kind of stunning reversal is typical of what Jesus does. He shakes the foundations of people with whom he speaks to move them from curiosity to commitment.

"Give me this water so that I won't get thirsty and have to keep coming here to draw water," she replies.

"Go call your husband and come back." Wow! Another major reversal in topics to raise the conversation to a deeper level. Be careful lady. Jesus is about to draw you into the inner circle of truth.

"I have no husband," she replies, her cheeks flushed as she speaks.

"You are right when you say you have no husband. The fact is you have had five husbands and the man you now have is not your husband." We don't know whether she was widowed or divorced five times, but we do know that she is currently living in sin. The man she's living with is not her husband.

Notice the meager attempt to change the topic. The truth is too hot for her so she moves to a safe topic and Jesus lets her go there. She compliments him. "Sir, I can see you are a prophet. Answer this question for me: 'We Samaritans worship on this mountain, but you Jews teach that we should worship in Jerusalem.' " She's stalling, and he knows it, but he temporarily goes along with her. Jesus discusses the place and nature of true worship with her. No one has ever talked to her like this before now. She's experiencing the courtesy of Christ.

That courtesy must have moved her deeply. She looks into his eyes, expecting to find condemnation for her sexual sins. Instead, she finds an invitation to believe in the Messiah. "I know that Messiah is coming," she says. "When he comes, he will explain everything to us." She wants to talk more about the idea of the Messiah.

Duck — here it comes, in no uncertain terms — his reversal touches her heart.

"I who speak to you am he."

Jesus' disciples return and are shocked that Jesus is talking about religion with a woman, a Samaritan woman at that. Meanwhile, the shady lady from Samaria crosses the line into commitment.

Commitment
The level of commitment of this Samaritan woman must have been quite low at first, like the commitment of the woman who touched Jesus' robe in hopes of healing. The woman who touched Jesus' robe started with a view of Jesus, which was near magic. The shady lady from Samaria started by picturing the Messiah as a soothsayer who could see her past and present. The courtesy of Christ means that he will start with us wherever we are. Commitment to Jesus Christ means giving up control of your life. That's a scary thing. For most people, commitment happens gradually; for her it happens instantly.

As the Samaritan woman dashes into town to tell everyone about Jesus, she comes to a deeper commitment. As she becomes an enthusiastic witness for Christ, her faith grows. That's true for all of us. If we have some experience of God and keep it to ourselves, it will probably fade. As we share what God has done, we grow.

She goes into Sychar, the Samaritan town near Jacob's well. There she tells everyone she meets, "Come, see a man who told me everything I ever did. Could this be the Christ?" They come to meet Jesus out of curiosity. Like the woman, they soon are moved to a deeper level. They listen to Jesus speak. Jesus sees they are ripe for the harvest. The invitation to become disciples goes out. The gospel of John reports, "... Because of his words, many more became believers."

Then they say to the woman, "We no longer believe just because of what you said; now we have heard for ourselves, and we know that this man really is the Savior of the world." Notice the shift from curiosity to commitment.

Confirmation students often go to class because mom and dad say they should. They sometimes get confirmed because they know it is the right thing to do, but they are far short of commitment to Christ. Sometimes, like the people of Sychar, as adults they cross the line from coming because someone tells them they should, to seeing for themselves that Jesus is Lord and Savior and making a personal commitment to him. Sometimes they arrive where they started in Baptism and know the place for the first time. They taste the wonder of eternal life again for the first time.

How do we try to teach our children about Christ? We take them to Sunday school and church services. We pray with them at home. We talk to them about faith in God. When the right time comes, we make sure they go to confirmation classes and we try to get them involved in the youth group. In other words, they come to some kind of faith in God because of what we say and what the Sunday school teachers say and what the pastor says and what the youth leaders say. How do these children come to the place where they say with the people of Sychar, "We no longer believe because of what you said; now we have heard for ourselves, and we know that this man really is the Savior of the world"? That's the difficult challenge for Christian parents.

The answer is that we, like the shady lady from Samaria, can only provide the context for our children to make a commitment to Jesus Christ as Lord and Savior. We can point to the one who alone gives life, but we can't guarantee that anyone will be a Christian. That's the work of the Holy Spirit.

Many Christian parents feel guilty when their children don't turn out to be Christians as adults. Sometimes that is because the example has not been good. More often, the reason is that the children have not made the journey from curiosity to commitment.

In *Song Of Assents*, E. Stanley Jones tells about his early Christian life. He was converted under the influence of the Reverend Robert J. Bateman, a strong man of God with a strong faith. As a youngster, Jones imitated what he saw in Bateman. Then he discovered the pastor had weaknesses. His idol had clay feet. It shocked Jones, but he saw a double truth: 1) his faith had been more in Bateman than in Jesus and 2) God uses imperfect people to lead people to faith.

Jesus is perfect. Robert Bateman was imperfect, but he was a great witness for Christ. Aboard a ship that was going down, Bateman helped the women and children to get aboard the life-boats. He then led the singing of "Nearer My God To Thee" as the *Titanic* slid into the icy waters of the North Atlantic.

We just witness to the good news in Christ. God, the Holy Spirit, leads people to commitment and real faith in Jesus Christ. The Holy Spirit also leads us into Christian community.

Community

The people in Sychar must have been excited after spending two days listening to Jesus speak. They were sad when he announced he was leaving. They had been transformed by him. How could they get along without him? That's how people felt when they met Jesus.

That's also how the apostles felt when Jesus announced that he was going to leave them. But he quickly added, "I will not leave you as orphans ... All this I have spoken while still with you. But the Counselor, the Holy Spirit, whom the Father will send in my name, will teach you all things and will remind you of everything I have said to you" (John 14:18-26). He also said, "It is for your good that I am going away. Unless I go away, the Counselor (the Holy Spirit) will not come to you; but if I go, I will send him to you" (John 16:7).

Jesus left the people in Sychar, but he gave them the Holy Spirit and the Spirit-filled community called the church that they might be sustained. In that community of faith, they continued their Christian growth. The Christian church is not primarily an organization, but a living organism for the spiritual growth of believers. Luther puts it this way:

> *I believe that I cannot by my own understanding or effort believe in the Lord Jesus Christ my Lord, or come to him. But the Holy Spirit has* called *me through the gospel,* enlightened *me with his gifts, and* sanctified *me in true faith. In the same way he* calls, gathers, enlightens, *and* sanctifies *the whole Christian church on earth, and keeps it united with Jesus Christ in the one true faith.*[2]

The Apostles' Creed teaches that the holy catholic church is the communion of saints. Saints are forgiven sinners. Forgiveness comes through the preaching of the word and the sacraments of Baptism and Holy Communion. In this church we commune with God and one another. We hear the word of God preached and taught. We experience the mutual consolation of God's people. We enter into selfless service of others in need. These are the ways of Christian growth.

The people of Sychar went through the grief of loss when Jesus left. So did the apostles. But they had to find their strength in Christian community. So do we. It is one thing to feel the movement of God creating trust in your heart. It is another to maintain that trust. It is one thing to have faith; another to be faithful. Faithfulness involves community. In his departure from Sychar, Jesus laid down one of the most important of spiritual principles. We Christians need one another and we experience Christ through one another. Dependence on Christ as Savior continues for a lifetime, but it includes interdependence on one another.

You can't be a Christian just because your parents were Christians. You can't be a Christian because your grandmother was a saint or because your grandfather was a pastor. As someone has put it, "God has no grandchildren, just children." Each generation must rise anew to call on his holy name and participate in Christian community in order to reach others for Christ.

You can't be a Christian just because at one point in time you went through a dramatic conversion experience. That experience may have been genuine, but it must be refined and extended in the Christian community where we receive Word, sacraments, and fellowship to sustain our faith. There must be a continuing conversion of the church and all its people.

The shady lady and the people of Samaria teach us that we can rediscover faith in Christ in the Christian community and know the place for the first time.

---

1. T. S. Eliot, "Little Gidding," *Four Quartets* (New York: Harcourt, 1943).

2. Martin Luther, *The Small Catechism* (Minnesota: Augsburg Fortress, 1979), p. 14.

Questions For Your Personal Consideration And/Or Group Discussion

1. Can you identify the ways in which parents and other people tried to help you find faith in God?

   • When you were a child?
   • When you were a teenager?
   • As an adult?

2. Can you identify your spiritual journey in terms of curiosity, commitment, and community?

3. If you are in a class or a small group studying this material, discuss the ways other people in your group help you grow spiritually.

4. Why do churches have difficulties in holding teenagers when confirmation classes are over?

5. What happens to our human tendency toward despair at the stages of curiosity, commitment, and community?

Chapter 5

The Eternal Now

John 3:36; 5:24; 6:47

According to the fourth gospel, John the Baptist said, "Whoever believes in the Son *has* eternal life ..." (John 3:36).

Jesus made this astounding claim himself: "I tell you the truth, whoever hears my word and believes him who sent me *has* eternal life ..." (John 5:24). Jesus also said, "Whoever believes *has* eternal life" (John 6:47).

Notice, these statements are present tense. Those who believe in Jesus Christ *will have* eternal life in heaven when they die. That's true enough, but the fourth gospel says, it's not big enough. Eternal life begins in the here and now. Those who believe in God through Jesus Christ *have* eternal life now, while they are alive.

To be sure, eternal life in the here and now is incomplete and imperfect. After all, we are still sinners, even when the Holy Spirit moves us to faith in Christ in this life. To be sure, at best, what we have here is an intimation of what we will have in heaven. Here we have previews of coming attractions; there (in heaven) we get the real thing. Here we have a foretaste; there we go to the great banquet. The point is eternal life begins here and now. We don't have to wait until we die or the world comes to an end to get in touch with it. With real faith in Jesus Christ, we move from death to life in anticipation of the full eternal life we will have when we die and join God in glory.

Whenever we look at Bible verses, it is good to consider the context in which they are found. Sometimes the context is revealing. That is certainly true of the "eternal now" statements in the fourth gospel.

John The Baptist Testifies About Jesus

In the third chapter of John we read about Nicodemus and the challenging statement of Jesus, "No one can enter the kingdom of God unless he is born of water and the Spirit" (John 3:5). We also encounter Jesus' words about the heart of salvation: "For God so loved the world that he gave his one and only Son, that whoever believes in him shall not perish but have eternal life" (John 3:16). Then Jesus warns: "Whoever believes in him is not condemned, but whoever does not believe stands condemned already because he has not believed in the name of God's one and only Son" (John 3:17).

After the encounter with Nicodemus, the incomparable invitation to eternal life, and the warning of condemnation to those who turn down the invitation to life, Jesus goes into the countryside where some new disciples are taught and baptized. The fourth gospel mentions that John the Baptist is also baptizing (John 3:22-23). While John is baptizing, an argument with the religious leaders breaks out about ceremonial washing. The Baptist's disciples are concerned that people are starting to go to Jesus for Baptism instead of coming to him.

In answer, John points away from himself. He points to Jesus as the one from above. "The one who comes from heaven is above all," he says (John 3:31). "The Father loves the Son and has placed everything in his hands" (John 3:35). In other words, the Baptist insists that he is not the Messiah. He's just a pointer to the one who saves.

That's the context of the words of John the Baptist, "Whoever believes in the Son *has* eternal life, but whoever rejects the Son will not see life, for God's wrath remains on him" (John 3:36). In other words, a person who has not yet come to faith in Jesus as Lord and Savior is dead. Only one who comes to saving faith is alive. Whoever rejects the Son experiences God's wrath.

70

God's wrath needs to be understood in the light of his holiness. We who are unworthy of him because we are not holy, are given a chance to leave this state of a dead and dull existence and come into the rich and blessed life of a child of God. The new life (eternal life) is only possible because God sent his Son out of love to save us. Let me put it another way.

People call you by your name (Mary, Sam, or whatever your name is), but you are not yet who you were intended to be until you cross that line between eternal life and eternal death. You can only cross that line by faith in Christ. You are Almost Mary or Almost Sam before you cross that line or when you cross back into the territory of unbelief. When you believe in the Lord, you really are who you were intended to be — Mary or Sam. On the one side, you are not what you were intended to be (that's called death); on the other side, you are who you were intended to be (that's called life).

That's the testimony of John the Baptist. Jesus says the same thing.

Life Comes Through The Son

Jesus said, "I tell you the truth, whoever hears my word and believes him who sent me *has* eternal life and will not be condemned; he has crossed over from death to life" (John 5:24).

Again the context of the verse is important. The context here, like in John 3:36, is an argument with Jewish leaders (apparently the Pharisees and Sadducees), this time about Jesus' authority and identity. Jesus heals a lame man at the pool of Bethesda on the sabbath day. The Jewish authorities, disturbed by this breaking of the sabbath restrictions, want to know by what authority Jesus does this (John 5:1-16). "Just who do you think you are?" they are saying.

In this context, Jesus tells them that God is his Father. The temperature of the confrontation rises to white heat when Jesus makes this claim. They claim he is making himself equal to God.

Jesus takes on the challenge by replying he can do nothing by himself. It is God who is working through him. "For just as the Father raises the dead and gives them life, even so the Son gives

71

life to whom he is pleased to give it" (John 5:21). The argument is raised to an even hotter level by this assertion. The red-face religious leaders don't know what to do with this upstart. That's why they think he will have to be killed to shut him up (John 5:18).

Then Jesus speaks directly about what these enemies, like all people, must do to cross the line into eternal life: "I tell you the truth, whoever hears my word and believes him who sent me *has* eternal life and will not be condemned; he has crossed over from death to life" (John 5:24).

In other words, Jesus is saying, "You leaders are not only wrong; you are walking and talking like you are alive, but inwardly you are spiritually dead." I'd say that's a rebuke of the first order! But we lose the full meaning here if we only consider Jesus' rebuke of stubborn, devil-possessed religious leaders of long ago and far away.

The challenging invitation of Jesus is given to all. By faith in Jesus Christ you can cross from less than you were intended to be to what God had in mind for you when you were born — eternal life in the here and now and in the hereafter. That's what the kingdom of God is all about.

The kingdom of God will come in the future with power and perfection. When the world ends and Jesus returns to reign as Lord of all, the kingdom breaks in with all its fullness. Here and now, by faith in the Lord, we can cross into the kingdom by having a relationship with the one and only God. We aren't all we should be. We aren't all we're going to be. However, we are different than we used to be — before we were transformed by the renewal of our spirits by the Holy Spirit.

Jesus is saying, "The kingdom is *coming in the future*, but I want you, my disciples, to start living as if it has already arrived by doing the kind of things you see me do: Forgiving your enemies, acting with selfless service, knowing that your real home is not here on earth, but in heaven. With my coming as the Word made flesh, I have made it possible for you to have a new quality of life as Christians *now*."

That's why Jesus taught us to pray: "... Thy kingdom come. Thy will be done on earth as it is in heaven."

In theology, this emphasis on the eternal now is called *realized eschatology*. Eschatology has to do with matters related to the end of the world and Jesus' reign as Lord of heaven and earth. Realized eschatology means that Jesus is Lord now. It's just a matter of people letting God be God and trying to live under the lordship of Jesus Christ.

In John 6:47, Jesus repeats this emphasis on the eternal now. "I tell you the truth, he who believes *has* eternal life." This time the context is a speech about the bread of life. "I am the bread of life," Jesus says (John 6:48).

In other words, eternal life comes to us in the here and now as well as in the hereafter. We have this eternal life through faith in Christ. The bread of life is given as a gift of the Holy Spirit. The bread of life sustains us in good times and bad times, even the worst times as we approach the dangerous state of despair. The bread of life is given to us in the sacrament of holy communion (John 6:52-59). In this sacrament we get a foretaste of the full eternal life that awaits believers when they die.

Get up high like an eagle and see the possibilities for this life and the next life.

Questions For Your Personal Consideration And/Or Group Discussion

1. Read the "eternal now" passages in the gospel of John (and their contexts):

   a. John 3:36 (and 3:5-35)
   b. John 5:24 (and 5:1-23)
   c. John 6:47 (and 6:48-59)

   What do you make of these verses?

2. Discuss this statement: "Any old religion won't do, even when people are sincere and good people. Humanism (doing good without God) won't do, either. God alone decides who goes to heaven and hell. That's not our job. Our job is to witness for Christ."

3. Read Acts 1:7-8. Consider the following exercise:

   a. Jerusalem was the place where the disciples were when they heard these words about being witnesses for Christ. Think of home.
   b. Judea was the country around and including Jerusalem. Think of neighborhood.
   c. Samaria was the territory of the outsiders and strangers. Think of strangers and people who are different than you are.
   d. The ends of the earth meant that disciples were to witness without limit to the ends of the earth. Think of missionaries.

   What are your personal areas for witness to the "eternal now" in Christ in your places of Jerusalem, Judea, Samaria, and the ends of the earth? Remember, when people are nearing despair in their lives, their extremity can be God's opportunity.

Chapter 6

The Great I AM

John 8:12; 8:58; 6:35; 10:11; 10:7; 15:5; 14:6; 11:43

In this chapter we will deal with these eight I AM verses in the gospel of John. In addition, we will look at an I AM verse from Exodus and three I AM verses from the book of Revelation.

"I AM WHO I AM"

In Exodus we hear the story of God calling Moses to save his people who are in bondage in Egypt. After Moses reluctantly agreed to go, he asked for God's name so that he could tell the people who sent him.

> God said to Moses, "I AM WHO I AM. This is what
> you are to say to the Israelites: 'I AM has sent me to
> you.' " God also said to Moses, "Say to the Israelites,
> 'The Lord, the God of your fathers — the God of
> Abraham, the God of Isaac and the God of Jacob —
> has sent me to you.' This is my name forever, the name
> by which I am to be remembered from generation to
> generation."   — Exodus 3:14-15

Let me paraphrase the words of the ancient story of Moses and the Great I AM. A bush was burning on a mountain called Sinai, near the plains of Midian. Moses watched in wonder. The bush was not consumed. Then he heard a voice: "Take off your shoes. The ground on which you stand is holy ground." Out of respect

75

and reverence, Moses took off his shoes. "Moses, I want you to go down to Egypt and free my people."

Moses replied, "I can't go. I'm not the man for the job."

"Moses, I will go with you."

"I just can't do it."

"Moses, you will be my spokesman."

"I can't speak for you. I'm not eloquent. I'm no public speaker."

"I made your tongue. Do you think that I can't give you the ability to speak for me?"

"I'm afraid. I just don't see how I can do it."

"Moses, I will give your brother, Aaron, the words. He can speak for you."

"Since you put it that way, I guess I have no choice. But who shall I tell the people you are? They will ask me what your name is."

"Tell them I AM WHO I AM sent you."[1]

We don't know the full meaning of this name God gave to Moses. Perhaps God was trying to emphasize that he is the one who has no beginning and no ending, the one who created all things, the one who will be there at the end of time. We don't know all that "I AM" means, but we do know that it means God is in control and we are called to submit to his will. That's what Jesus is talking about in the gospel of John when he uses the name I AM for himself.

"I Am The Light Of The World"

In John 8 we read that Jewish leaders were in conflict with Jesus about the control issue.[2] They tried to trap him by bringing a woman caught in adultery to him. "Tell us, should we stone her or set her free?" they asked. If Jesus said, "Stone her," they would point out that in contrast he had previously been preaching compassion. If Jesus said, "Free her," they would respond that he was making himself greater than Moses, for the law taught that an adulteress should be stoned. A perfect trap to show that Jesus was not as powerful as people were saying. However, Jesus trapped them in their own trap. Quietly, Jesus took his staff and wrote in the sand. What did he write? We don't know. Maybe he wrote the names of the people there who had committed adultery. Looking up, Jesus said, "Let him who is without sin cast the first stone."

Stunned sinners quietly dropped their stones and left. Jesus looked into the eyes of the woman who was being used as a pawn in the power game. "Has no one condemned you?" he asked.

"No one," she replied, trembling.

"Neither do I condemn you. Go now and leave your life of sin."

Conflict about power and control continues in John 8. People who set the traps and get caught in the traps they set don't easily forget how they have been embarrassed. In verse 12, we read that Jesus used the name I AM for himself.

"I am the light of the world," Jesus said. "Whoever follows me will never walk in darkness, but will have the light of life" (John 8:12). That lit another fuse. The tension rose another notch with the Pharisees who must have been thinking, *Using God's name for yourself are you? Pretending to be the light of the whole world? Just who do you think you are? Bragging about your own power? We've got you this time.*

The conflict multiplied when Jesus told the Pharisees they were spiritually blind and in bondage. "You do not know me or my Father," he said (John 8:19). Many people in the crowd in the temple rejoiced at these words, but the Pharisees seethed. It got worse.

Jesus said, "If you hold to my teaching, you are really my disciples. Then you will know the truth, and the truth will make you free" (John 8:32).

"So now you are saying we are slaves?" they asked cynically. "How can you say, 'We shall be set free'? We are Abraham's children and have never been in bondage to anyone."

"Before Abraham Was, I AM"

To add fuel to the fire, Jesus not only said that the Pharisees were blind and in bondage to sin, he said they were demonic liars. "You belong to your father, the devil" (John 8:44). "The devil is a liar and you are liars," Jesus is saying. Then he went on to answer the Abraham question. "Abraham rejoiced at the thought of seeing my day; he saw it and was glad" (John 8:56).

77

The Jewish leaders who were at fever pitch yelled back sarcastically, "You are not yet fifty years old ... and you have seen Abraham!" (John 8:5).

"Jesus said to them, 'Very truly, I tell you, before Abraham was, I am' " (John 8:58 NRSV).

At this, they picked up stones to throw at him because of his claims, just as they had picked up stones to throw at the adulteress in the beginning of John 8. The ultimate insult! I AM is God's name. Rage turned to physical violence. But Jesus slipped through the confused crowd before the Jewish leaders could get to him and kill him.

The first chapter of John's gospel tells us, "In him [the Word made flesh] was life and that life was the light of men. The light shines in the darkness, but the darkness has not understood it" (John 1:4-5). Again John says, "He [the light of the world] was in the world, and though the world was made through him, the world did not recognize him. He came to that which was his own, but his own did not receive him" (John 1:10-11).

Here in John 8 we see how the people in darkness resent and reject the light of the Great I AM. Jesus' rejection by stubborn, blind sinners runs parallel to the story of stubborn rejection by sinners in the exodus out of Egypt when God sent manna from on high.

"I Am The Bread Of Life"

In John 6:1-15 we read about the feeding of 5,000.[3] Earlier in chapter 6, Jesus tells his followers about the meaning of heavenly nourishment. He says that as Moses fed the people in the wilderness with manna, so he now feeds them with heavenly food. Whereas the manna in the Old Testament story perishes, the bread of life Jesus gives is imperishable.

In this context, Jesus told his followers, "I am the bread of life" (John 6:35). This statement caused grumbling among some of Jesus' followers. As there was grumbling and murmuring in the wilderness against Moses and God, there was grumbling and murmuring against Jesus because he said, "I am the bread of life."

It is in this setting of conflict that John's gospel pictures Jesus giving the promise of the holy sacrament: "I tell you the truth, unless you eat the flesh of the Son of Man and drink his blood, you have no life in you" (John 6:53). The words of institution don't appear in the gospel of John. Instead, in the fourth gospel we have these words about the necessity of eating and drinking the body and blood of the Lord and the bold and beautiful promise that Jesus will be present in the holy sacrament. "I am the bread of life," he says. In addition, Jesus speaks of himself as the good shepherd.

"I Am The Good Shepherd"

In the tenth chapter of John we read that Jesus told his followers about his continuing care for them and us. "I am the good shepherd. The good shepherd lays down his life for the sheep" (John 10:11). These words remind us of the divinity of Jesus since he uses the name of God for himself. They also tell us of how the Great I AM lowers himself to the depths by dying on the cross for the sins of all his sheep.

We, the sheep who so easily go astray, are the recipients of the greatest sacrifice ever made, Jesus' death on the cross that we might have life. In Isaiah 53:6 we read about the meaning of the cross: "We all, like sheep, have gone astray, each of us has turned to his own way; and the Lord has laid on him the iniquity of us all."

In Psalm 23 we hear about the way God defends his sheep. "For thou art with me; thy rod and thy staff, they comfort me" (Psalm 23:4b RSV). The rod of the ancient shepherd is a baseball-bat-like club, used to beat off the wolves. The staff of the shepherd is used to keep the sheep in the flock. The shepherd would gently tap a sheep on the backside as he started to stray. The shepherd knows what the sheep don't know. Unless sheep stay in the flock, they have no chance of survival. If a sheep goes astray, the good shepherd leaves the 99 and seeks diligently for the one lost sheep. On finding him on a ledge of a cliff, the shepherd reaches down with the crook of the staff and rescues the sheep. The rod and staff of the good shepherd are wonderful instruments for our defense according to this Old Testament psalm.

The New Testament adds another instrument of God used for defense against our enemies: the cross of Christ, which defeats sin, death, and the devil. That Jesus died for us on the cross means that he looks down from the cross and says to each of us, "I'd rather die than give you up." That's how much Jesus, the good shepherd, cares.

Jesus not only speaks of himself as the good shepherd; he also says he is the gate of the sheep.

"I Am The Gate Of The Sheep"

In ancient times, the shepherd would lie down in the open space of a pen where the sheep would be kept overnight. The shepherd's body was the door or gate of the sheep pen. In order to get out, the sheep would have to literally jump or crawl over the shepherd's body. In order to get in, wolves would have to jump over the shepherd.

That Jesus is the gate of the sheep (John 10:7) means that he knows better than we know that we must stay together as a flock. Nocturnal exits are not allowed; no slipping away because we don't know better. Jesus watches and protects, even in the darkest times.

That Jesus is the gate of the sheep means that with his rod he beats off the wolves that would attack us at our most vulnerable times, the shadowy, dark places of the night. The enemy is stronger than we are, but the good shepherd is stronger than the enemy. We must stay close to the Lord, as close as a branch is to a vine.

"I Am The True Vine"

In John 15:5, Jesus tells us how close we are to him. "I am the vine; you are the branches. If a man remains (other translations read 'abides') in me and I in him, he will bear much fruit; apart from me you can do nothing." Attached! That's as close as you can get.

Some years ago, my wife and I bought a refrigerator. On the back of the refrigerator we found a warranty tag that read, "Void If Detached." Something like that is happening in these verses. Unless we stay attached to Jesus Christ, our lives are null and void. Whatever we do apart from him is zilch.

Since Jesus is the true vine, what does he expect from us? Nothing and everything. Dwelling, or abiding as some translations put it, is a matter of doing nothing. Dwelling is a matter of achieving nothing but receiving everything. To dwell in the Lord means we don't have to accomplish anything. From the cross Jesus said, "It is accomplished." Our salvation is accomplished by the action of Jesus on the cross. Our part is just to remain attached to the vine in which we have life. As a branch of a grape vine is invalidated if detached, so we are invalidated if we try to live detached to the Lord. We shrivel up and die, like a branch cut off from its source of life. If attached, we can accomplish great things for the Lord.

Our part is to stay close to God like a little girl crossing a busy street with her father. We had three daughters. When they were little, they would go anywhere with me, even across a busy highway, as long as I held their hands. If they let go and tried to make it on their own, they would never make it. Our part in salvation is just to hold on tight to the Father's hand that holds our hand. Our part is to follow where God leads.

"I Am The Way, The Truth, And The Life"

The apostles who first heard these words were like children who had wandered away from a parent in a large crowd. Jesus had told them repeatedly he would be going away. They couldn't imagine life without him. The very thought of his leaving made them feel estranged, detached, confused, and anxious, like orphans.

Peter asked, "Where are you going?" (John 13:36).

"Where I am going, you cannot follow now, but you will follow later," Jesus answered (John 13:37). Then he went on to explain that in his Father's house there are many rooms. "Do not let your hearts be troubled. Trust in God: trust also in me" (John 14:1). "You know the way to the place where I am going" (John 14:4). Thomas then asked, "How can we know the way?"

That's the context for Jesus' profound statement: "I am the way, the truth, and the life. No one comes to the Father except through me" (John 14:6).

Our good works don't get us to heaven. If good works could get us to heaven, why would Jesus have to die on the cross for us?

Our religion doesn't get us to heaven. There were all kinds of religions in Jesus' time. He clearly taught that something more than man-made religion is necessary for salvation. Man-made religion is our attempt to get to God. All such attempts ultimately fail. We are lost and condemned sinners if left on our own. God must find us and save us. That's what he does in the person of Jesus Christ. That's what the cross means.

It's not our job to judge who goes to heaven and who goes to hell. That's God's job. It isn't our task to condemn others or to act superior because we are Christians. We are called to be humble witnesses to Jesus Christ, the way, the truth, and the life. We are called to point people to the one and only Savior and to their real home, which is with God.

Jesus told the apostles that their real home was heaven. He promised them that one day they would join him there. In the meantime, he promised that he would send them his comforter, the Holy Spirit, to guide them through life (John 14:25-27). That's our assurance as well. This earth is not our real home. Heaven is where we will live eternally. Here on earth, we have temporary residences. In this life, the comforter will guide us in the ways of Christ. In the sufferings and joys of this life, the Holy Spirit points us to the one who brings eternal life.

When it comes to salvation, Jesus is not one choice among many. He isn't even the best choice. He's the only choice. Jesus, the Great I AM, said he was the way, the truth, and the life.

"I Am The Resurrection And The Life"

In John 11:25, we read that Jesus made this statement to his friend, Martha, at her brother, Lazarus', funeral. Soon thereafter he went to the tomb of Lazarus and called out in a loud voice, "Lazarus, come out" (John 11:43). Jesus, the Great I AM, not only said the words about resurrection. He performed the act of raising a man from the dead.

A mother living in a tenement house went shopping for groceries. While she was in the store, a fire engine raced by. Feeling panic she cried out, "Is the fire engine going to my home?" She had left her baby asleep in her bedroom. *I'll only be gone a few minutes*, she had thought.

Forgetting the groceries, she ran home, only to discover her building was burning like a matchbox. Rushing to the fire chief, she cried out, "My baby's up there."

"Sorry, lady," he replied. "It would be suicide for anyone to go up there now."

A young fireman heard the conversation. "Chief, I have a little baby at home, and if my house was on fire, I'd want someone to go up and save my baby. I'll go." The young fireman climbed the stairs; he got the baby and threw her out the window into the rescue net. The house collapsed around him and he burned to death.

Twenty years later at a graveside, a twenty-year-old woman was sobbing softly. Before her, at the head of the grave, was a statue of a fireman. A man stopped by and asked respectfully, "Was that your father?"

"No," she replied through her tears.

"Your brother?"

"No, this is the man who died for me."

At a much deeper level, we can say about Jesus, "He's the one who died for me. He's the one who died to give all of us the gift of resurrection from the dead."

"I Am The Alpha And The Omega"

Tradition says that the apostle John wrote the book of Revelation, as well as the gospel that bears his name. In Revelation 1:8, we read, "I am the Alpha and the Omega, says the Lord God, who is, and who was, and who is to come, the Almighty."

Revelation 21:5-6 gives us the same name, I AM, in a little different setting.

> *He who was seated on the throne said, "I am making everything new!" Then he said, "Write this down, for these words are trustworthy and true." He said to me: "It is done. I am the Alpha and the Omega, the Beginning and the End. To him who is thirsty I will give to drink without cost from the spring of the water of life."*
> — Revelation 21:5-6

Again we see reference to God, the Great I AM, in Revelation 22:12-13:

> *"Behold, I am coming soon! My reward is with me and*
> *I will give to everyone according to what he has done.*
> *I am the Alpha and the Omega, the First and the Last,*
> *the Beginning and the End."*
>
> — Revelation 22:12-13

We conclude this chapter on the Great I AM with the reference to the one from whom all things come and to whom all things go. In the first passage, Revelation 1:8, the Alpha and Omega is called the almighty. In Greek, this word is *pantokrator*, the one who is over us. If we don't worship the almighty, we will put someone or some thing in his place. There's no such thing as an atheist. Anyone who rejects the one true God will put something else in his place. One man put it this way:

> *Unless that which is above you,*
> *controls that which is within you,*
> *that which is around you, will.*
>
> — Anonymous

In the second passage, the Alpha and Omega is pictured as the one who quenches our thirst. Nothing else will satisfy. As we saw in our study of the story of the Samaritan woman, Jesus promises living water. Our ultimate thirst is for God. That thirst is quenched only in adoration of the almighty.

The third passage indicates that the Alpha and Omega is coming back soon. To come back soon doesn't necessarily mean within the next few days, months, or years. It means that we know how the story will end, so we live our lives in the light of that knowledge. This reference is an invitation to live with the assurance that in the end, the Judge of heaven and earth will make all things right. Adoration of the almighty in John's heavenly vision is an invitation to lose ourselves in worship of the one true God, through Jesus Christ, our Lord in this life and the next.

I have a friend who loves to read novels, especially mysteries. She has a strange habit. She reads the end first. Then she goes back to page one and starts to read how the author works things out to get to the conclusion.

While that is a strange way to read a mystery novel, it is precisely the right way to read the mysteries of this life. Start at the end; then live out all the various ups and downs of life in the light of God's ultimate rule and judgment. That's the way to live the Christian life. That's the way to handle the suffering that comes to every life. That's the way to avoid despair. That's the eagle's eye view of life in the gospel of John.

---

1. Originally the Hebrew language had no vowels, only consonants. For fear of offending the Lord, the Jews did not pronounce the name he gave to Moses. It is impossible to know precisely what vowels should be added to the consonants we have. For some years, scholars thought the proper name for God was Jehovah. In modern times most scholars think the proper name God gave to Moses in Exodus 3 is Yahweh.

2. Some ancient manuscripts do not have John 7:53—8:11.

3. The text mentions 5,000 men. Women and children were likely present as well, but were not in this count.

Questions For Your Personal Consideration
And/Or Group Discussion

1. The concept of the Great I AM is an abstract idea. Are there stories in this chapter that help you personally make the concept more real? Have you heard other stories that make almighty God more understandable to you?

2. Consider the story of Adelaide Pollard:

    Adelaide was at the end of her rope. She was discouraged and depressed. She felt like a failure. She was sure God had called her to be a missionary in Africa, but she had failed to raise the money she needed to go. Adelaide was far short of her goal.

    In desperation, she went to a prayer meeting at her church. At the prayer meeting, an older woman prayed, "Lord, it really doesn't matter what you do with us — just have your way with our lives." Adelaide was stunned by the trust this woman had in God. She realized that by contrast, she had almost been telling God what he should do in her life. She went home from the prayer meeting and opened her Bible to Jeremiah 18:1-6, a passage in which the prophet describes himself as a clay pot with God as the potter.

    That night, Adelaide Pollard composed a hymn.

    > *Have thine own way, Lord, have thine own way.*
    > *Thou art the potter, I am the clay.*
    > *Mold me and make me after thy will*
    > *While I am waiting — yielded and still.*

3. Which of the I AM sayings is your favorite? Why do you like it so much?

Chapter 7

Full Life And Joy

John 10:10; 15:11

Some years ago, while driving through Yellowstone National Park, I heard a frustrated young man who was upset by the traffic congestion break the second commandment as he asked a question. "For Christ's sake, what's going on here?" he shouted. While it is certainly not my intention to promote the taking of the name of God in vain, there is another way to ask that question. For the sake of Jesus Christ, what is going on here on earth?

When God sent his Son into the world, he intended that through him we would have abundant, full lives. He intended that we experience joy in its fullness. Jesus said, "I have come that they may have life, and have it in full" (John 3:10b). He also said, "I have told you this so that my joy may be in you and that your joy may be complete" (John 15:11).

Full Life

It is always important to consider the context of a Bible verse. When Jesus spoke of his intention that we have full, abundant lives, he was explaining the meaning of his being the good shepherd and the gate or door for the sheep (John 10:7-9; 10:11-18). He contrasted himself with thieves who come only to steal, kill, and destroy (John 10:10a) and hired hands who run away when trouble comes (John 10:12-13). In other words, Jesus protects his sheep. Others use and abuse the sheep and refuse to stay with the sheep when they are faced with the attacks of the beasts of this world.

The people of God are like so many sheep who need God's protection and salvation. Jesus Christ gives us what we need. "We like sheep, have gone astray, each of us has turned to his own way; and the Lord has laid on him the iniquity of us all" (Isaiah 53:6).

Sheep are not smart enough to stay out of danger. They try to scatter and go off on their own, only to discover that they cannot exist outside the flock. The good shepherd protects his own with his rod and staff (Psalm 23:4b). The rod is a baseball-bat-like club that the good shepherd uses to beat off the wolves of prey. The rod is used to keep the sheep from going astray. The shepherd who cares about his sheep taps them on the backside to keep them in the flock. Should one sheep go astray, the shepherd seeks him out. If he finds the sheep on a ledge of a cliff, he places the crook of the staff under his belly and lifts him back to safety.

That Jesus is the gate or door of the sheep literally means that like shepherds of old, when night falls, the good shepherd lays his body down in the opening of the crude pen for the sheep. In order to get out, a sheep must go over the body of the shepherd. For a wolf to get in, that beast will have to contend with the shepherd.

That's the context of Jesus saying, "I have come that they may have life, and have it to the full." Full or abundant life means trusting the protection and salvation that Jesus provides.

Let me paraphrase this verse negatively and positively. First, the words of Jesus mean that we can't have full life without him. All other attempts at a meaningful life fall far short of what God intends for us. We are not fully what we were intended to be unless and until we come to trust Christ as our good shepherd. Try hedonism ("Life is pleasure"), humanism ("Do good without God"), or a man-made religion or philosophy like "New Age" (which is not new and certainly doesn't usher in another age) and you will fall far short of the meaning life is supposed to have.

Second, what Jesus means here is that when you come to trust him, you experience protection, salvation, and the abundant life you were intended to know. The good shepherd lays down his life that you may have a full life. The concept we translate "full life," or "abundant life" means "rich beyond your imagination; complete in every way, ordinary life with a plus, thus extraordinary."

A young artist came to a master and sought his approval on a painting he had done. The master studied the painting for a while. Then he said, "Amplius. Amplius. Make it larger. Larger." The master artist wasn't talking about the size of the picture, but the quality of development of the idea behind the picture. Likewise, when God looks at our petty efforts at finding a meaningful life, he says, "Amplius. Amplius. Make your idea larger by coming to new life through my beloved Son."

Some people tell us that they have tried the Christian way and it hasn't worked. G. K. Chesterton said a generation ago, "The Christian ideal has not been tried and found wanting. It has been found difficult and left untried."

The difficult part is to trust Christ as Lord. That means we seek to live under his rule, try to do what he says, and acknowledge he is wiser than we are. The shepherd is smarter than the sheep.

The difficult part is to trust Christ as Savior. We may think we can get ourselves out of the situations we create by going astray, or the bad things that happen to us even when we are trying to do the right things. We can no more save ourselves than we can lift ourselves out of a chair by the hair of our heads. God knows us better than we know ourselves. He knows that full life can only be experienced through his Son.

Leslie Brandt has paraphrased Psalm 139 in a revealing way.

> O God, you know me inside and out,
>   Through and through.
> Everything I do,
>   every thought that flits through my mind,
>   every step I take,
>   every plan I make,
>   every word I speak,
> You know, even before these things happen.
> You know my past;
>   you know my future.
>
> Your circumventing presence covers my every move.
> Your knowledge of me sometimes comforts me,
>   sometimes frightens me;
> but always it is far beyond my comprehension.[1]

Full Joy

Full life means having our joy fulfilled. Jesus said, "I have told you this so that my joy may be in you and that your joy may be complete" (John 15:11). Again, the context of this verse is important for us to consider. Just before speaking these words, Jesus told his disciples that they must dwell in him like a branch dwells in a vine and thus bear much fruit. "Apart from me, you can do nothing," he says (John 15:5).

Full joy is not achieved. It is received by dwelling in Christ. Complete joy is received not by seeking it for itself, but as a by-product of full trust in the source of life. C. S. Lewis, the English intellectual who was converted to Christianity as an adult, titled his biography *Surprised by Joy*.

Full joy spins out of full faith in Christ as Lord and Savior. Full joy is to be contrasted with both no joy and partial joy. Frederick Nietzche, the atheist philosopher who grew up in a Lutheran parsonage, once said, "You Christians are going to have to look and act more redeemed if you want me to believe in your redeemer."

Full joy is different than the partial happiness experienced by natural man when things go right. The joy of seeing a child at play, two older people walking hand in hand in the park, or hearing good news that "our ship has come in financially" are good and natural times of happiness. The joy of Jesus includes earthly joys, but goes far beyond them. Natural happiness comes and goes. Full joy is abounding and lasting.

Christians are not perfect. All of us have our down times, our times of difficulty and depression. Full joy in the sense that Jesus meant it, doesn't mean that we completely overcome sin and always smile. It means that we are given the capacity to overcome those things that threaten to be our undoing by the strength that Christ supplies as we dwell in him. When you are magnetically drawn into the kingdom of God, it is like stepping into another world.

Helen Keller, the little girl who was deaf, blind, and unable to communicate in normal ways, stepped into another world through the persistent efforts of her teacher, Anne Sullivan.

In her early childhood years, Helen was the captive of her surroundings. Each room was full of hostile dangers. Helen was a captive within herself, cut off from significant sharing. As a captive, she was filled with fears and rage. She was unable to know the meaning of things. She didn't understand other people. She was unable to comprehend the connection between words and what they described.

Anne Sullivan changed all this. She taught Helen to react to various stimuli, even as we do. But Anne wasn't satisfied with that. She didn't believe that Helen was beyond the freedom and dignity of knowing the meaning of things and their names. She sought the key that would help Helen see the relationship of things and people. "One word and I can put the world in your hands," Anne cried out to Helen.

For Helen, the word that opened life with a new meaning was W-A-T-E-R. "It's water," Anne shouted. "The thing has a name." That opened the floodgates to a new life for little Helen.

The floodgates to a new life can be open for us as well. That's what the words of Jesus in these passages about full life and full joy mean.

These words have a meaning. The meaning opens up life to a fullness we were intended to know.

Spell it out in your hand. Feel. See. Hear. Touch. Discover. The name is J-E-S-U-S. In him is life and joy. Since God sent his Son into the world, since Jesus died for us, since he told us that we can have a full life and full joy by faith, the kingdom of God is near to us, within our grasp the power to overcome despair is close.

J-E-S-U-S. Say it out loud. Spell it out on your hand. Write it down. Pray that the meaning sinks in.

For the sake of Jesus Christ, what's going on here in your life?

----

1. Leslie Brandt, *Psalms Now* (St. Louis: Concordia, 1973), p. 211.

Questions For Your Personal Consideration And/Or Group Discussion

1. The context of John 10:10 is John 10:7-9 and 10:11-18. What does it mean that Jesus is the good shepherd and the gate (door) of the sheep?

2. The context of John 15:11 is John 15:5-10 and 15:12-17. What do these verses mean? How are they connected with John 15:11?

3. What things of this world do people seek to bring happiness to them?

4. In seeking the things of this world, in what ways do people find fulfillment and joy? In what ways do the things of this world fall short of meeting our needs?

5. As outsiders look at the church, do they see reflections of Christ's life and joy?

Chapter 8

The Place

John 14:1-2

On the Thursday before he died, Jesus met with his apostles in the home of John Mark near Jerusalem to celebrate Passover. There he instituted the Lord's Supper. He also gave his farewell address. That farewell address included words of encouragement about the place that has been prepared for us. "Do not let your hearts be troubled. Trust in God, trust also in me. In my Father's house are many rooms; if it were not so, I would have told you. I am going there to prepare a place for you" (John 14:1-2).

As I write this chapter, I am in my home on a hill in Encinitas, California, three blocks west of the Pacific Ocean. My study faces east, looking down on a beautiful valley and lagoon. More than any other house where we have lived, this house is a peaceful "place" for us.

As I was writing yesterday, a mother dove was trying to build a nest in a small space between rafters on our porch. She was busy, coming and going, carrying one twig at a time. She was singing all day long, trying to build a place for her family. By the end of the day, she was exhausted and disgusted. It was no use. The space was just too small. She flew away. She had failed to build a place for her family.

At a much higher level, by the time he reached the upper room that Thursday in Holy Week, Jesus was exhausted. He was not only bone tired with what he had done. He knew what lay ahead —

the indescribable suffering and death on the torture rack called the cross. Yet, he did not give up. He promised that he would see his way through whatever lay ahead and prepare an eternal place for his family. "I go to prepare a place for you," he said.

In anticipation of getting a better picture of the place prepared for us in the hereafter, it may be helpful to think about significant places in the here and now.

Places In The Here And Now

As I have spoken at various conventions, conferences, retreats, and workshops around the country, I have often used a spiritual exercise I call "Imagination." Go with me on a journey of the imagination. Assume a comfortable position.[1]

Relax any part of your body that may be tense. When you are ready, mentally, get up and leave this room. In your imagination, go to any place you'd like. It should be a significant place for you. For now, don't take anyone with you. You are in your special place alone.

Where are you? What does it mean?

What objects do you see? Pick out three or four objects and study them carefully. Touch them, gently and lovingly, if you wish. If you had to eliminate all but one of these special objects, which would you eliminate? Which would you keep? Now, dispose of all but one. What do you see?

In your special place there are special sounds. What do you hear? If you had to eliminate all but one sound, what would you keep? Now, keep just one sound. What do you hear? Let yourself be bathed in this one sound.

Next, imagine that you could bring one person with you in this place. Whom would you choose? Why that person?

If you could talk about just one topic with that special person, what would you talk about? Now, talk to that special person about anything on your mind. What does it mean?

Many people who have used this spiritual exercise say that they went somewhere near water — a lake, a river, a stream, or the ocean.

Some people have reported that they went to a cabin, a garden, a forest, a mountain, a church, or their home. Some report they saw trees, sky, birds, animals, or flowers. For some, the sounds they heard were of birds, moving water, the wind blowing through the trees, or music. The people they brought include a mother or father, a spouse, a child, a friend, or a pastor. In some cases, the person selected was dead. Since this exercise is in the imagination, there are no restrictions.

People have reported that in the exercise they talked about love, problems, joys, resentments, unforgiven sins, experiences they shared, places they have gone, secrets they have shared or want to share, death, and heaven.

The place you go in this exercise may very well be a special place for you in the here and now that points you to a better understanding of the place Jesus has prepared for you in eternity. In this special place, there is nothing we have to do. It is a place to be. The person you talked to may very well be a "little Christ" for you, someone who in your mind helps you understand God better by listening to you and talking to you, letting you be who you are.

In order to understand something about the place Jesus has prepared for us in eternity, it helps to have significant places and people in our life journey here on earth. In his book, *A Place For You*, Paul Tournier, the Swiss physician-counselor, says that having a place to be where you don't have to do anything is key to understanding the meaning of place in John 14. Having a significant person you can talk to helps us overcome the problems, which otherwise can overwhelm us. In this place, you can get an eagle's eye view of your life.

Dr. Tournier tells the story of one of his young patients who had a neurosis *failure*. The young man said, "Basically, I'm always looking for a place — a place to be." Disharmony between his parents had a harmful effect on him. In his family there was a stark contrast between expressed beliefs and violent actions. There was little communication. In his mind, he tried time and again to reconcile with his parents, but never succeeded. As he got older, he took his mother's side out of pity, but that only antagonized his father more. At the time of the divorce, the young man's anxiety was acute. He was cut off from his father and powerless in the face of his mother's problems.

When his father remarried, the tension increased. The young man failed at school, unable to concentrate. He had no friends, only acquaintances. He felt paralyzed emotionally. He tried work, but that didn't satisfy. He tried religion, but made no real connections. Dr. Tournier tried to help him, but felt that he could not get through. The young man wandered aimlessly from one group to another.

"What he was looking for was a real community where he was accepted," wrote Dr. Tournier. "He was looking for a place to be."[2]

Shouldn't the church be such a place for people? For some it is. Others, especially those who feel like outsiders, often fail to make the connection between church and a significant place to be. Jesus created the church to be a colony of heaven, a preview or a foretaste of the place to come. That's one of the reasons why small groups are so important in our churches today. Some people come and go through the doors of the church without ever knowing that the church is the fellowship or community of believers, a significant place to be. Some will only make that connection as they participate in small groups with concerned Christians. Small groups are a way for people to grow spiritually and relationally.[3] Small groups are not a panacea for what is wrong with congregations today, but these groups can make a major difference for many people who need a place to be.

The books I have written have promoted small group ministry by including questions at the end of each chapter as discussion starters and tips for small group leaders. Jesus said, "Let not your hearts be troubled ... I go to prepare a place for you." God prepared us for that place by giving us opportunities for Christian fellowship in this life. Small groups in the church provide the context for that fellowship.

The Place In The Hereafter
When Jesus spoke the words of John 14:1-2, he was preparing his followers for his death. He wanted his disciples to know that they could overcome their grief by staying close to God through

the power of the counselor (John 14:16, 25) and the fellowship of other believers. "I will not leave you as orphans," he said (John 14:18). Even in death, Jesus promises we will not be left bereft, desolate, comfortless, or alone.

Jesus prepared a place for us in heaven with the Father and the family of believers. By trusting him, we have the assurance that God the Father will receive us into the ultimate place to be — heaven.

Eight-year-old Jimmy really enjoyed playing outdoors with the other children. When he got sick, he wasn't able to go out and play anymore. His mother took him to a doctor to see what was wrong. "I'm sorry to tell you this," the doctor told her privately, "but your son has an incurable disease. It's just a matter of time before he dies."

The young mother was devastated. Not only did she have the grief of losing her son, but she couldn't think of any way to tell him. She stewed and brewed about it, but nothing came to her. She talked to her husband. He didn't have any ideas, either. The mother was wiped out like a dish by the impending death of their son.

One day, as she and her son were sitting beside a window, looking longingly out the window at the other children playing, she read to her son the story of King Arthur and the Knights of the Round Table. She read about the battles and how some of the knights died in battle. Suddenly, Jimmy asked her, "Mom, what is it like to die? Does it hurt?"

She excused herself quickly, using the excuse that she was going to get some milk and cookies before she answered his questions. "Lord, what can I say? How can I tell him?" she prayed. Then it dawned on her.

"Jimmy, do you remember when you used to play so hard that you would come home exhausted and just flop down on the couch in the front room?"

"Yeah, Mom, I remember."

"Do you remember how the next day you would wake up in your own room?"

"Sure, Mom, I remember."

"You got from the wrong place to the right place because you have a strong father who carried you to your own room. Jimmy, that's what it's like to die. We fall asleep in the wrong place and wake up in our own room, a special room that God, the Father, has prepared for us. We get to the place God has prepared for us because we have a strong Father who loves us and carries us there."

Jimmy died a week later, at peace with God and comforted by the words of Jesus, "Do not let your hearts be troubled. Trust in God, trust also in me. In my Father's house are many rooms; if it were not so, I would have told you. I am going there to prepare a place for you."

Saint Paul described the glory to come as we go home to God like this:

> *No eye has seen,*
> *no ear has heard*
> *no mind has conceived*
> *what God has prepared for those who love him.*
> — 1 Corinthians 2:9

Don't despair. God has prepared a place in heaven for you.

---

1. When using this spiritual exercise in a group, it is helpful to have the people close their eyes as the words are read.

2. Paul Tournier, *A Place for You* (New York: Harper and Row, 1966), pp. 9-12.

3. For information on how to start small groups and keep them going, see Ron Lavin, *Way to Grow! (Dynamic Church Growth Through Small Groups)* (Lima, Ohio: CSS Publishing Company, Inc., 1996).

Questions For Your Personal Consideration And/Or Group Discussion

If you are not reading this chapter as a part of a group, you are encouraged to find someone with whom to share these questions for discussion.

1. Read and discuss John 14:1-2.

2. Have one person read the spiritual exercise called "Imagination." Others should keep their eyes closed as this exercise is read. Talk about the individual answers to the questions about significant places, sights, and sounds. Talk about the significant people that participants brought to their special place and what they talked about.

3. How can this exercise help someone to avoid the pitfalls of despair?

4. Read 1 Corinthians 2:9 and discuss.

5. Often the words of scripture, even famous verses like the ones we are studying, seem distant or even dull as we read them. Read and discuss the following story:

   A young woman was reading a book she felt was dull. She just couldn't stay with it. Several days later she attended a party and met a dashing and gifted young man. Everyone was attracted to him. When she got an opportunity to speak to him later that night, she asked, "What do you do for a living?"
   "I'm a writer," he replied.

When she got home that night, she glanced at the book by her table and saw the author's name. The book was written by the fascinating man she had just met. She stayed up all night reading the fascinating book. Now she knew the author.

Chapter 9

Prayer Power

John 16:13-24; 17:1-21

Does prayer really work? There are many people outside the church and some within the church who believe the answer to that question is, "No," or "Maybe, but I don't know how to make it work." In some cases, the reason that prayer doesn't work is that it is viewed as a kind of Aladdin's lamp from which we are supposed to get what we want, when we want it, how we want it. In other cases, people have earnestly prayed and felt that God either doesn't care or he's asleep.

Many people outside the church have told me over the years, "I'm not interested in church or God. I had a crisis; I prayed and God wasn't there."

On the other hand, many mature Christians have told me that it was the crises in their lives that caused them to deepen their faith. "I prayed to God and he was there. He got me through the crises."

What's the difference between these two groups? The difference is that for church people, other Christians were there. The support and intercessory prayers of other people were the way God was present for believers in crises. In other words, God often answers our prayers through the support he sends through other people.

A man once told his pastor, "I'm never coming back to church again. Recently, I was lost in the cold wilderness of Alaska. In desperation, I prayed to God, but he never answered me. What kind of God is that?"

"But you are here," said the pastor. "What happened? You didn't die."

"God was of no help at all. An Eskimo passed by and saved me," the man replied.

Dangerous and distorted ideas about prayer were present in the man's approach. He approached prayer in a highly individualistic way. He expected God to magically pop out of the clouds and save him. When God didn't show up as expected, he missed the way that God saved him. The man's understanding of prayer was self-centered and manipulative. There are many like him who lose faith because of distorted expectations about prayer. Let's look for the Eskimos God sends to us.

Moving From Childishness To Maturity

John 16 describes a crisis in the lives of the apostles. Jesus had told his followers he was going to die. They couldn't believe it. They wouldn't believe it. Jesus had told them that he would send them the counselor (the Holy Spirit) as an advocate to get them through their grief and the troubled times ahead (John 15:26-27; John 16:5-11). Then he added,

> *A woman giving birth to a child has pain because her time has come; but when her baby is born she forgets the anguish because of her joy that a child is born into the world. So with you: Now is the time of grief, but I will see you again and you will rejoice, and no one will take away your joy. In that day you will no longer ask me anything. I tell you the truth, my Father will give you whatever you ask in my name. Until now you have not asked for anything in my name. Ask and you will receive, and your joy will be complete.*
> — John 16:21-24

Jesus tried to move his apostles from childishness in prayer to mature prayer. It is safe to say the apostles prayed that Jesus would never die as he predicted. They insisted that he stay with them. They couldn't wait for the glory Jesus promised. That would come later, but they wanted it now. The desire for instant gratification is childishness.

Maturity means we are willing to wait. A woman giving birth to a child has to learn to wait. Everything depends on the right time. Psalm 130:5 says, "I wait for the Lord, my soul waits and in his word I hope." That's what mature prayer is all about — waiting for the Lord.

An eight-year-old boy went to the movies. There he heard a demanding man say to a beautiful woman, "I vant, vhat I vant, vhen I vant it." He didn't know what it meant, but it sounded good. He went home and tried it on his seven-year-old girlfriend. "I vant, vhat I vant, vhen I vant it," he said. She replied, "You'll get vhat I got vhen I get it."

Maturity means waiting. It also means learning to give up control. A woman in childbirth is totally out of control. Understandably, she wants to get away from the pain, but she is not able to control the situation. "So with you," Jesus tells his followers. "Now you have grief at my death, but I'm coming back. It's out of your control, but when you understand that, you will submit to my Father's will. Then you will have your joy complete, like a new mother seeing her child for the first time."

Maturity means having a higher perspective (an eagle's view) on what happens to us. Jesus knew the bigger picture. He would leave his followers and by his departure they would grow from spiritual children to adults. As they grew in their trust in God, they would learn to pray according to God's will, like Jesus himself prayed. He taught them to pray to God, "Your will be done on earth as it is in heaven." That's a hard lesson to learn for all of us.

Mark Twain has one of his characters, Huck Finn, lose faith in prayer, because as he says, "I tried it. I asked for a bike. I asked several times. It never came. I gave up. No more prayin'." That's a magical view of prayer. For Huck, prayer was something like Aladdin's lamp. When you rub the lamp, you're supposed to get what you want, when you want it, how you want it. When Jesus said, "Ask and you will receive," what he had in mind was prayer by mature disciples in harmony with God's will, not prayer as a way to get God to do what we want him to do.

Maturity in prayer means discerning the difference between what we want and God's ways. What we want and what God wants for us may be miles apart. That's why we need the gift of discernment.

Young king Solomon prayed a mature prayer to God for guidance. He wanted to be a good king. We pick up the story in 1 Kings 3:4.

> *The king went to Gibeon to offer sacrifices, for that was the most important high place, and Solomon offered a thousand burnt offerings on that altar. At Gibeon the Lord appeared to Solomon during the night in a dream, and God said, "Ask for whatever you want me to give you."*
>
> *Solomon answered, "You have shown great kindness to your servant, my father David, because he was faithful to you and righteous and upright in heart.*
>
> *"You have continued this great kindness to him and have given him a son to sit on his throne this very day.*
>
> *"Now, O Lord my God, you have made your servant king in place of my father David. But I am only a little child and do not know how to carry out my duties. Your servant is here among the people you have chosen, a great people, too numerous to count or number. So give your servant a discerning heart to govern your people and to distinguish between right and wrong. For who is able to govern this great people of yours?"*
>
> — 1 Kings 3:4-9

Notice, Solomon clearly stated he was out of control. The people were God's people, not his people. He confessed he was not able to rise to the task of governing by his own strength. He sought to justly administer his task of leadership, but he knew he could do it by his own power. That's when he discovered the power of mature prayer. He prayed for wisdom in order to be a godly leader within the faith community.

> *The Lord was pleased that Solomon had asked for this. So God said to him, "Since you have asked for this and*

104

*not for long life or wealth for yourself, nor have you
asked for the death of your enemies but for discernment in administering justice, I will do what you have
asked. I will give you a wise and discerning heart...."*
— 1 Kings 3:10-12

That's what Jesus was telling his apostles in John 16. "Pray for mature leadership skills when I am gone. Pray for openness to the Holy Spirit. Pray for perseverance. Pray for a willingness to do God's will. Learn to wait for the Lord. Learn to be patient to discover how God will act. Learn to give control to God. Let God be God." You can count on God's saying, "Yes," to prayers like that. God sometimes says, "Yes," to our prayers, sometimes, "No," but most often, "Wait."

James 1:4-5 puts it this way: "Perseverance must finish its work so that you may be mature and complete, not lacking anything. If any of you lacks wisdom, he should ask God, who gives generously to all without finding fault, and it will be given to him."

Selfish motives give rise to immature prayer. Prayer doesn't get me what I want on my time schedule. With biting accuracy, James 4:2b-3 describes the situation of many who pray childishly: "You do not have, because you do not ask God. When you ask, you do not receive, because you ask with wrong motives, that you may spend what you get on your pleasures."

In John 16, Jesus tells his followers to cross the high barrier from the immature demands in prayer to a mature prayer life centered in the desire to do God's will. In this more mature way of thinking, you can ask God for anything and have your joy complete.

In John 17, Jesus adds another dimension to the power of prayer. That dimension is community.

Moving From Self-Centered Manipulation To Community

Continuing his insistence that he will soon die and the apostles will have to carry on his mission, Jesus offers prayers to his Father for the apostles and for those who will follow them in the Christian community.

Father, the time has come. Glorify your Son, that your Son may glorify you ... I have revealed you to those whom you gave me out of the world. They were yours; you gave them to me and they have obeyed your word. Now they know that everything you have given me comes from you. I gave them the words you gave me and they accepted them. They knew with certainty that I came from you, and they believed that you sent me. I pray for them. I am not praying for the world, but for those you have given me, for they are yours ... Holy Father, protect them by the power of your name — the name you gave me — so that they may be one as we are one....

My prayer is not that you take them out of the world but that you protect them from the evil one ... My prayer is not for them alone. I pray also for those who will believe in me through their message, that all may be one.   — John 17:1-21

Jesus prayed for the apostles to be one. He prayed that for all of his disciples over the ages. He prayed that we would be one with God and one another. He prayed that we might be lifted from our small perspectives to larger ones. He prayed that we might come to see the importance of his dying for us on the cross. He prayed that we might be a Christian community in which people could grow from being children needing spiritual pabulum to mature, growing disciples. He prayed that we might learn to pray for one another, leaving our own little worlds and entering the world of other people in need.

Understandably, children may be selfish in their prayer life. They may ask for things like bikes and toys. God understands that they are at an age when requests like these are an expression of their limited point of view. When selfish petitions come from adults, we have a different situation altogether. Jesus expects that we grow into a community of people having mutual consolation for one another. He expects us to leave childish ways and rise to maturity. "When I was a child, I talked like a child, I thought like a child, I reasoned like a child," Saint Paul wrote. "When I became a man, I put childish ways behind me" (1 Corinthians 13:11). Maturity means not trying to be the center of everything. Maturity means growing in community. Maturity means not trying to manipulate God according to our will. Maturity means getting an eagle's eye view of reality.

Bishop William Temple observed: "The essential act of prayer is not the bending of God's will to ours — of course not — but the bending of our wills to his. The proper outline of a Christian's prayer is not, 'Please do for me what I want,' but 'Please do in me, with me and through me what you want.' "[1]

In the high priestly prayer of Jesus in John 17, the emphasis is on disciples becoming one with God, as Jesus himself was one with God. This high-sounding principle of being one with God in actual practice means coming under the lordship of Jesus Christ. After a lifetime of trying to run the show ourselves, we see that life is God's show and he alone can run it. That is what *Jesus as Lord* means. The corrective for trying to run the show and acting like the universe revolves around us is the Christian community where Jesus is Lord. In Christian community we learn that instead of playing God ourselves, maturity means letting God be God.

In *The Taste Of New Wine*, Keith Miller speaks of his conversion to Christianity in terms of the breaking of his will to conform to God's will. "God wants your will; and if you give him your will, he'll begin to show you life as you've never seen it before."

In the high priestly prayer in John 17, Jesus is teaching us to submit our wills to God. Manipulation, in the negative sense, is the opposite of submission to God's will. In the positive sense, manipulation simply means good management, but in the negative sense it means trying to control people by using unfair or insidious means so as to serve our own selfish purposes. Highly individualistic and self-centered people live and pray as if the universe revolves around them. That's the opposite of Christian community.

In the high priestly prayer of Jesus in John 17, the emphasis is on disciples being at one with one another. That means unity, not unanimity, but unity. We are not called to have unanimous opinions. We are called to listen to one another, to minister to one another, to care for one another in selfless ways in what Luther called the mutual consolation of the saints (forgiven sinners). That's what unity means. William Barclay describes Christian unity like this:

> *What was that unity for which Jesus prayed? ... It was a unity of love for which Jesus prayed, a unity in which men loved each other because they loved him, a unity based entirely on the relationship of heart and heart ... Only love implanted in men's hearts by God can tear down the barriers which they have erected between each other and between their churches.*[2]

In the high priestly prayer, Jesus prays that we might not be caught in the demonic divisions of the world. Unity is the opposite of demonic division. Jesus says, "My prayer is not that you take them out of the world but that you protect them from the evil one" (John 17:15). The evil one is the prince of lies. The evil one is the promoter of division. The evil one is the devil, who rejoices when we undercut one another, gossip about one another, murmur against God and godly leadership, or try to manipulate one another with insidious motives.

Does prayer really work? Of course it works when we understand the purpose of prayer is to give glory to God, who has our best interest in mind, who seeks unity with us and among us, who never has insidious motives in dealing with us, and who loves us more than we love ourselves.

In the high priestly prayer, Jesus prayed for us to be a Christian community because he loves us. It is good to remind one another of this

- when someone in the Christian community is depressed;
- when someone is having a hard time with children or parents;
- when someone's fondest dreams are shattered;
- when disappointment and discouragement come;
- when friends become enemies;
- when hard decisions need to be made; or
- when a loved one is sick or dies.

Does prayer really work? Yes, when we follow the lead of our Lord and offer intercessory prayer for one another. More good is accomplished by intercessions and other prayers by mature Christians in community than any of us can imagine.

Unbelievers say, "A crisis came. I needed God; he wasn't there." Mature believers say, "I needed God and he was there." The difference for believers is that God's people are there in time of need and God uses them to make his will known. Christians recognize the Eskimos God sends. Unbelievers don't.

About the power of prayer, Christians can say what Marco Polo said about his journeys. In the fourteenth century, when Marco Polo came back from his explorations with stories of the wonders of the world he had seen, many did not believe his tales. They accused him of lying and exaggerating. When he was dying at age seventy, they asked him to confess his lies, since he was about to face God. His answer was, "I never told the half of it."

Don't despair. Learn the meaning of mature prayer.

---

1. Bishop William Temple, *Readings in St. John's Gospel* (London: McMillan, 1955), p. 305.

2. William Barclay, *The Gospel of John*, Vol. 2 (Philadelphia: Westminster, 1975), p. 218.

Questions For Your Personal Consideration And/Or Group Discussion

1. Read Matthew 7:7-12 and comment on prayer as
   Asking _____
   Seeking _____
   Knocking _____

2. Consider this model for prayer — ACTS
   A - Adoration
   C - Confession
   T - Thanksgiving
   S - Supplication

3. How is the Serenity Prayer of Alcoholics Anonymous like the prayer of Solomon in 1 Kings 3:5-11 and the advice of James 1:4-5?

   ### The Serenity Prayer
   God, give me the courage *to change those things I can change,*
   the serenity *to accept the things I cannot change,*
   and the wisdom *to know the difference.*

4. What difference does it make for your suffering that Jesus prayed for you?

Chapter 10

Conflict Between Light And Darkness

John 18:1 – 19:16

From the beginning, the gospel of John promises, "The light shines in the darkness, but the darkness has not overcome it" (John 1:5). Yet, as we look at the dark garden betrayal, the six illegal trials, and the corrupt sentencing of Jesus in John 17-18, we must honestly confess, "It doesn't seem to be so."

The story of conflict between light and darkness in John 18 and 19 apparently gives a decided edge to the darkness. A major battle between Jesus and the powers of the high priests on the one hand and the Roman governor on the other climaxes with Jesus being led to the cross outside Jerusalem. As we read these verses, we can almost hear a satanic voice-over saying, "Gotcha. Now, free yourself from this vise grip if you can. "This story of conflict ends with an apparent tragedy. A good man is led away to be crucified. Of course, we know the rest of the story, but for a few minutes step into the heart of darkness with Jesus. Easter will mean more to you if you do.

The Insidious, Inciting Incident
Judas, one of the original twelve apostles, betrays Jesus in a garden on the Mount of Olives. He betrays him with a kiss. To have a friend turn against you is one of the most unnerving experiences in life.

The temple soldiers move in at the signal of the kiss. Jesus asks, "Who is it you want?"

"Jesus of Nazareth," the soldiers cry out.

"I am he," Jesus says. "Let the others go."

Simon Peter, the big fisherman, grabs a sword and strikes the high priest's servant, cutting off his right ear.

Jesus rebukes his friend, "Peter, put away your sword. Shall I not drink the cup the Father has given me?"

Then, another gospel tells us, Jesus heals the servant's ear.

The soldiers arrest Jesus, bind his hands, and take him to Annas, the former high priest.

While this is the insidious, inciting incident for the darkest days in human history, William Barclay, the Bible commentator, insists there is still light in the situation as we look at the character of Jesus in the beginning of the end of his life.[1]

First, this garden scene shows his courage. Jesus demanded to know who the temple guards were seeking. When they answered, he clearly identified himself, unafraid of the power of the soldiers. Understanding the courage of a real leader is integral to grasping the meaning of this story.

Second, Jesus shows his authority. At his arrest, Jesus is a single, lonely, unarmed figure facing a group of armed men, yet, as John tells the story, Jesus is clearly in command of the situation.

Third, the story of the garden arrest shows that Jesus chose to die. We know his power from other parts of the Bible. He could have walked through the waiting soldiers just like he walked through the hysterical mob in Nazareth when they tried to push him over a cliff. Instead, he lets himself be bound, arrested, and led away to face trial.

Fourth, in this incident we see Jesus' protective love. "Take me. Let these men go." Even though he knows they will betray him, he protects his friends.

Fifth, we see light in the darkness of this story because it shows Jesus' utter obedience. "The Father has given me this cup to drink. Shall I not drink it?" He is determined to be faithful unto death.

The character of Jesus shines in the darkness of betrayal and arrest, but what will happen as the story twists and turns in the dark, illegal trials ahead?

The Progressive Complications Of The Six Trials

The mockery of justice in the six trials of Jesus is part of the dark backdrop for this second act in the drama of the last days of Jesus. One writer estimates the arrest took place about 1 a.m. The first trial took place at 2 a.m. at the house of Annas, the former high priest. The second unofficial trial took place around 3 a.m. in the home of Caiaphas, the high priest and son-in-law of Annas. The third trial, a formal hearing before the Sanhedrin, the seventy-man supreme court of the Jews, took place "when it was day" or about 6 a.m. The first interrogation by Pilate, the Roman governor, took place about 7 a.m. That was the fourth trial. Shortly thereafter, Herod, the tetrarch of Galilee, granted Jesus an audience, his fifth trial. When Herod sent Jesus back to Pilate for a sixth trial, it was about 8 a.m. A rush to judgment? You decide.[2]

A travesty of justice! Trials are held in the middle of the night and early morning with no reputable witnesses and no defense lawyers, on two different charges (blasphemy in the religious trials and that Jesus made himself king in the civil trials). To top off the travesty, Jesus is declared guilty, but never proven guilty. In the end, Pilate says he finds no guilt in him, yet Jesus was given capital punishment — death by crucifixion. The Roman governor caves into the demands of the mob. Is this justice?

Let's look closer at the six trials and see the conflict build and the complications compound. The first trial is before Annas, the notorious and malicious former high priest. Annas is the power broker of Jerusalem, known for his intrigue, bribery, and corruption. Among the Jews, Annas is the arch-collaborator with Rome.

When Jesus overthrew the money tables in the temple courtyard, he hit Annas where it hurts — in his money bag. Annas got his cut of these sales of sacrificial animals. Now is his time to get even with the man who had attacked the system that made the religious ruler rich. When you attack a man's vested interests, you can expect violent retribution. Now is the time to gloat over the capture of the man from Galilee. Before Annas, Jesus is condemned before he is tried.

Remember, it is about 2 a.m., a most unusual time for a trial. Annas is wide awake in anticipation of the arrest of this man deemed to be an enemy. John reports that Jesus says, "I have done everything in the open. Why question me? Ask those who heard me. Surely they know what I said." In other words, "Where are your witnesses?" For that question, Jesus got a sock in the face from one of the temple officials. Annas sends Jesus to the house of Caiaphas.

The gospels report that Peter is in the courtyard of the high priest. Three times he is asked if he is a follower of Jesus or even knew the man. Three times he denies it, the last time with a curse. As Jesus is led through the courtyard of the high priest, the cock crows,[3] a poignant moment in the tragedy of Jesus' last days. The Lord turns and looks straight at Peter. Peter remembers the words the Lord has spoken to him: "Before the rooster crows today, you will disown me three times." He goes outside and weeps bitterly (Luke 22:61-62).

The second trial is before Caiaphas, in his home. It's about 3 a.m. What a place and time for a trial! The gospel of John gives no details of this trial, but Matthew 26:57, 59-68 reports that Caiaphas and his friends in the Sanhedrin are busy trying to find false witnesses to testify against Jesus. Does this sound like the work of an impartial judge?

Jesus is led from the house of Caiaphas to the meeting of the Jewish supreme court. Caiaphas leads the unjust judgment at the third trial before the seventy-man court of elders called the Sanhedrin. The gospel of John doesn't report the details of the proceedings, but we get some of what happened from Luke 22:66-71.

Caiaphas and the other members of the Sanhedrin ask Jesus directly, "Are you the Son of God?"

Jesus answers, "You are right in saying I am."

"Condemned by his own words," they shout. "That's blasphemy!"

The Romans had taken capital punishment out of the hands of the Jews. The Jewish leaders want this ultimate punishment. Therefore, they lead Jesus out of the courtroom toward the residence of Pontius Pilate.

The fourth trial of Jesus is before Pontius Pilate "in the early morning," which means about 6 a.m. Pilate is irritated by the early morning demands. He is further irritated by the refusal of the Jewish leaders to defile themselves by entering the palace of a non-Jew. To satisfy their desire to be ceremonially clean, Pilate goes outside to where the Jewish leaders are gathered instead of having them come inside his palace. Crisply, coolly, he asks, "What charges are you bringing against this man?" We pick up the story of conflict between Pilate and the Jewish leaders in a paraphrase of John 18:30.

"If he were not a criminal, we would not have handed him over to you," the Jewish leaders reply.

Pilate says, "Take him yourselves and judge him by your own law."

"But we have no right to execute anyone," the Jewish leaders object.

Pilate goes back inside the palace, and asks Jesus, "Are you the king of the Jews?"

"Is that your own idea," Jesus asks, "or did others talk to you about me?"

"Am I a Jew? Your people handed you over to me. What is it you have done?" Pilate asks.

Pilate takes Jesus aside, in effect saying, "Let's get away from this mob. I'm tired of these priests. Let's talk about this man to man." He comes right to the point with his question about kingship.

Jesus answers Pilate's question with a question. "Are you really interested in the answer to your question, or are you just repeating words others have told you?" In other words, "If you really want to talk, I'm willing to do that, but if you are playing games, I want none of it." That sounds like Jesus is in control. Pilate notices the authority in the so-called criminal before him and dodges the question by indicating he wants no part of Jewish squabbles. "What have you done to cause all this hatred?"

Jesus answers the governor's question and shifts back to the kingship question. "My kingdom is not of this world. If it were, my servants would fight to prevent my arrest by the Jews. But now my kingdom is from another place." In other words, "My kingdom is heavenly, and no threat to Rome's secular rule." The subtle conflict between ruler and ruled expands.

"You are a king, then!"

"You are right. That's why I was born. Everyone on the side of truth listens to me."

"What is truth?" The question hangs unanswered in the air as Pilate comes to the conclusion that this heavenly king was no threat to him. Leaving Jesus inside, the governor goes outside and declares to the priests and their henchmen, "I find no basis for a charge against him." In essence, Pilate is saying, "This man is an innocent victim in your power struggle. You won't trap me in your schemes." Then an idea dawns on him. The ruler cynically states, "It is your custom for me to release to you one prisoner at the time of the Passover. Do you want me to release 'the king of the Jews'"? (John 18:39). An interesting move in the game of life and death, but they aren't going to fall for it.

"No. Not Jesus. Give us Barabbas."

The gospel of Luke (ch. 23, vv. 5-7) fills in the gap in the story of the fourth trial. The Jewish rulers insist, "This man from Galilee stirs up the people." Pilate sees another move in the power game the Jewish priests are trying to play. "Galilee, you say? We'll send him to Herod." A brilliant, political ploy. Roman.

The fifth trial is before Herod, the infamous Jewish ruler who had John the Baptist beheaded and had killed many members of his own family. Herod asks Jesus to perform a miracle to prove himself. Jesus gives no answers to the questions the ruler of Galilee fires at him. Herod mocks Jesus further by placing a royal robe on him and sends him back to Pilate.

The sixth trial is once again before the Roman ruler. Layers upon layers of complications and conflicts all come down to one question: "Pilate, what are you going to do with this man Jesus?" John reports that Pilate has Jesus flogged. The soldiers mock the Lord by placing a crown of thorns on his head. "Hail, king of the

Jews," they shout again and again as they strike him in the face. Pilate once more announces to the crowd, "I find no basis for a charge against him." The priests and their officials shout stridently, "Crucify! Crucify! Our law says he must die for he claimed to be the Son of God" (John 19:1-7).

Pilate returns to Jesus inside the palace, deeply disturbed by what he has heard, but now unable to get Jesus to answer his questions. "Don't you realize I have the power of life and death over you?" he screams.

"You have no power over me, except that given from above," Jesus says.

"Take him outside." Then Pilate once again tries to appeal to the crowd. "Here is your king." Feel the tension in the air as pitiful Pilate pleads with the mob. "Shall I crucify your king?" Feel the conflict as the crowd responds.

"We have no king but Caesar."

Pilate, the ruler, feels like a pawn in the game of conflict between the religious leaders and Jesus. In the struggle between light and darkness, Pilate tries to play on the side of light, but gets sucked into the darkness.

The Apparent Tragedy Of The Corrupt Sentencing

We have traced the story of Jesus' last days from the insidious incident of betrayal, through the progressive complications of the six trials. All this leads us to the corrupt sentence. John puts the apparent tragedy at the end of Jesus' life in simple terms: "Finally, Pilate hands him over to them to be crucified." After all these questions and all this game playing, after one power struggle after another, Pilate washes his hands of this matter and gives Jesus to the soldiers who take him to Golgotha, commonly called "The Place of the Skull."

Repeatedly, Pilate had said, "Jesus is innocent," but he doesn't have the courage of his convictions. He fears for his own reputation more than he fears God's wrath. In the last analysis, the Roman governor is a pawn in the hands of the prince of darkness and the corrupt high priests.

It is a tragedy that got worse when Jesus is crucified, but we know the rest of the story. The tragedy deepens in the horror of Calvary. But then, the story makes a shocking upswing, the ultimate reversal. The Roman ruler and Jewish rulers turn out to be victims of their own schemes. Jesus, the apparent victim, is the victor. John puts it this way: "The light shines in the darkness, but the darkness has not overcome it" (John 1:5).

What does this part of the drama of Christ have to do with us? What connection do we make with our lives? What difference does all this make?

Whenever we feel like victims, it is helpful to remember these dark days in the life of our Lord. It looks like there is no way out for Jesus. When it looks like we have no way out of our troubles, we can recall that God always has another move.

Since Jesus went through the darkest valley of shadows, we know that he understands our dark valleys. Since Jesus got through these darkest times, we can be confident that we can get through, even when faced with horrendous suffering and are tempted to fall into despair. We are not alone. There is always hope. When faced with the valley of the shadow of death itself, Jesus' message is, "I am with you. Don't despair. I'll meet you on the other side of death."

1. William Barclay, *The Gospel of John*, Vol. 2 (Philadelphia: Westminster, 1975), pp. 223-224.

2. Charles Swindoll, *The Darkness and the Dawn* (Nashville: Word, 2001), pp. 59-60.

3. *Op cit*, Barclay, pp. 346-347. William Barclay, the New Testament commentator, says that 3 a.m. was called "cockcrow" in Jerusalem. Roman guards changed places and a trumpet was sounded. It may have been that sound which Peter heard.

Questions For Your Personal Consideration And/Or Group Discussion

1. In your imagination, step into the character of Peter in the garden and in the courtyard of the high priest (threefold denial and Jesus' look). What do you feel?

2. Have someone read the six trials of Jesus out loud (pp. 113-114). Summarize what happened below.

Trial 1: estimated time 2 a.m., at the house of Annas, the former high priest

_____

_____

Trial 2: estimated time 3 a.m., at the house of Caiaphas, the high priest

_____

_____

Trial 3: estimated time 6 a.m., before the Sanhedrin

_____

_____

Trial 4: estimated time 7 a.m., before Pontius Pilate the first time

_____

_____

Trial 5: estimated time 7:30 a.m., before Herod, the ruler of Galilee

_____

_____

Trial 6: estimated time 8 a.m., before Pilate the second time

_____

_____

3. In your imagination, step into the character of Pontius Pilate. What's going on in your mind?

Chapter 11

"It Is Finished"

John 19:16b-42

The crucifixion of Christ is both strange and wonderful. It is strange because it is the most cruel and horrible punishment imaginable. It is a slow strangulation, like drowning for six hours. The lungs are slowly crushed as the weight is shifted from hands to feet and back again, time and time again. A strange death for the Son of God. Yet, when we focus on the crucifixion, we discover something wonderful for by that focus, we experience God's magnetism in drawing us to himself. Jesus said, "I, when I am lifted up from the earth, will draw all men to myself" (John 12:32).

Chapter 19 of the gospel of John is a strange and wonderful mixture of the brutal human suffering of Jesus and his divine perspective. The humanity of Jesus is dramatically portrayed by his concern for Mary, his mother, and John, his youngest apostle (John 19:26-27), and Jesus' cry to quench his thirst (John 19:38). The divinity comes through with the powerful word of triumph from the cross, "It is finished" (John 19:30).

The most powerful symbol of Christianity, the cross of Christ, is strange and wonderful. Some people trivialize the cross by using it as a trinket or a good luck charm. Strange. Many would be shocked if they arrived at church one day to find an electric chair over the altar, but that's what the cross means as it stands there, a reminder of the instrument of capital punishment in Jesus' day — strange.

Yet, this instrument of death invites us to come under its compelling influence and experience new life. Focusing on the cross of Christ can totally change a person's life. The cross of Christ is truly strange and wonderful.

A monk in the Middle Ages invited people to come to church for a special evening worship service during Lent. When the people arrived in the dark church, they noticed there was only candlelight. They could barely see the monk. He began by making the sign of the cross over the people. He said, "Remember." Then after five minutes of silence, the monk made his way to the altar area where he picked up a large candle and lit it from one of the altar candles. "Behold," he said in a loud, clear voice as he walked to the foot of the large crucifix on the front wall and held the lit candle there for twenty minutes. "Behold, what has been done for you," he said. Then he closed the service with one word, "Amen."

Join the journey to the foot of the cross where we will focus on the man who died there to give us life. Watch and listen as Jesus says in effect, "I'd rather die than let you go." Take the monk's words with you, "Behold what has been done for you."

In order to get the full impact of what happened that rainy Friday we call good, consider not only the three "words" of Jesus[1] from the cross from the gospel of John, but the four "words" from the other gospels as well. In your imagination, you are there.

"Father, Forgive Them,
For They Do Not Know What They Are Doing"

The soldiers are leading the way to Golgotha, the place of the skull. The first two criminals are nailed to their crosses. Listen to the screams of pain, cursing, and suffering. The crosses are dropped into the holes with a thud. The third man is being nailed to his cross, too. But reviling is not to be heard from his lips. There is a physical reaction to the nails meeting flesh, but no cursing. Before raising the cross to put it in the pre-dug hole in the ground, one of the soldiers pounds a placard to the top of the cross. The placard reads, "Jesus Of Nazareth, The King Of The Jews." The sign is written in Aramaic, Latin, and Greek.

Behold the words about Jesus the king of the Jews written in three languages. Aramaic, a dialect of Hebrew, represents the religion of the one true God. Latin, the language of the Romans, represents law, order, and authority. Greek is a sign of beauty in form and high thinking. The paradoxical meaning of the placard above the head of the crucified Christ is that here in this dying man is the consummation of these three great cultures. Behold what is happening here. The crucifixion spans these cultures. Jesus is the king of the universe, who has authority beyond the greatest powers of the world.

The third cross is dropped into the hole with a thud. The four soldiers gamble for the clothes of the criminals (John 19:23-24). Who gets first choice? Watch as each of the four soldiers gets one piece of clothing. One piece remains. Who will get the robe? The robe of Jesus is seamless. Is there a second meaning here? The robe of the high priest is seamless. The word "priest" in Latin is *pontifex*, meaning "bridge builder." This is the function of Jesus, our high priest, building a bridge between God and us, making the highest sacrifice. Behold. Jesus is fulfilling Old Testament prophecy, "They divided my garments among them and cast lots for my clothing" (Psalm 22:18).

Then Jesus speaks — beaten, bruised, and bleeding Jesus — innocent, tortured, and crucified Jesus. Maybe now the words of revenge, reviling, and cursing will come. These Galileans are tough, but finally he's breaking. Think again. Jesus says, "Father, forgive them for they do not know what they are doing" (Luke 23:34). Behold forgiveness.

Forgiveness, offered even to his enemies? Forgiveness is the theme on his lips in his dying hours. For the crowd at the cross — forgiveness offered. For the Roman soldiers and chief priests — forgiveness offered. For us — forgiveness offered. Saint Paul says that Jesus took our guilt and nailed it to the cross (Colossians 2:13-15).

We are stunned. The crowd is stunned. The two thieves on his left and right are stunned.

"Today You Will Be With Me In Paradise"

Listen, as the mocking crowd chants, "Save yourself! Come down from the cross if you are the Son of God! ... He saved others, but he can't save himself ... He trusts in God. Let God rescue him now if he wants him" (Matthew 27:39-44). Listen as the thief on Jesus' left hurls insults at him. "Aren't you the Christ? Save yourself and us" (Luke 23:39). Crucifixion brings indescribable pain. Who wouldn't want to be free from this suffering? Who could think of anything other than self at a time like this? Yet, the thief on the right, astounded by the manner of Jesus as he is being crucified, perhaps remembering the words of Jesus about forgiveness for those who don't know what they are doing, cries out against the self-centeredness of the man on the left. "Don't you fear God since you are under the same sentence? We are punished justly, for we are getting what our deeds deserve. But this man has done nothing wrong" (Luke 23:40-41). Then turning to Jesus, he says, "Jesus, remember me when you come into your kingdom." It's a remarkable turn from self to Jesus. It's a remarkable turn from physical suffering to spiritual matters. It's remarkable repentance.

When under extreme stress, some people look for one thing from God; some look for another. Some want God to bail them out of the mess they have gotten themselves into; others see what they have done for what it is and repent. The former are disappointed when they receive nothing; the latter are amazed when they receive more than they expect or deserve.

Listen as Jesus answers the thief on the right, "I tell you the truth, today you will be with me in paradise" (Luke 23:43). Behold the promise of heaven.

People ask about deathbed conversions: "Are they really possible? Is it possible to turn from a life of self-centeredness to God in our last hours on earth?" To be sure, some who say they are sorry for a lifetime of sins and ignoring God may be saying the words superficially, or out of fear of hell. To be sure, some may say the words, "I'm sorry," without changed hearts. To be sure, some may still be in the grip of self-centeredness in their so-called repentance. But, it is possible for a person to sincerely turn from self to God as he or she is dying. Behold the thief on the right.

124

Turning from the temptation of rationalizations, from trying to balance good deeds against evil deeds, from languishing in his sins, the thief on the right turns to Jesus. That's what repentance means: turning from self to Jesus.

In the first word from the cross, Jesus shows compassion for the crowd when he asks for forgiveness. In the second word from the cross, he shows compassion for the thief on the right by forgiving him on the spot and promising paradise. In the third word from the cross, Jesus shows compassion for his mother and the apostle John.

"Dear Woman, Here is Your Son ... Here Is Your Mother"

Jesus is slowly strangled by the process of crucifixion. As the pain of the iron spikes in his hands becomes too great, he lets the burden pass to his nail-pierced feet. When he can't stand the pain in his nail-pierced feet, he lets go and transfers the pain back to the hands, wrists, and arms. Back and forth — again and again — who could think of anything but the suffering? Behold selflessness.

When Mary approaches the cross with John, the youngest apostle who with the others deserted him during the garden arrest, Jesus shows compassion. Touching and tender concern for the welfare of his mother and friend is shown by the dying Savior.

Mary, who had humbly agreed to the use of her body for the birth of the Messiah; Mary, whose heart was broken when Simeon told of the forthcoming suffering of her son; Mary, who watched Jesus depart the carpenter's shop and his filial responsibility as the eldest son for a greater responsibility of salvation for those who would believe in him; Mary, who is shattered as she watches her son dying on the cross like a common criminal; Mary comes close to the cross and looks up into the eyes of her beloved son.

Understandably, Mary and young John are concerned for Jesus, but it is the concern of this dying man for them that fills us with wonder. In the midst of the cosmic battle between good and evil, we watch in amazement at the tender mercy of Jesus, concerned for his mother and his youngest follower. From the cross, Jesus says, "Dear woman, here is your son ... [John] here is your mother" (John 19:26b-27).

We are amazed by the compassion of the first three words of Jesus from the cross. We are awestruck in a different way, as we hear the last four words of the cross describing the work of salvation for the world. The fourth word from the cross is the cry of dereliction.

"My God, My God, Why Have You Forsaken Me?"

Watch. It's noon. It starts to rain. Then it pours. It is as if the heavens are crying. Darkness comes over the land. A bolt of lightning rips across the dark, angry heavens. Listen. Thunder roars in the heavens. After hours of physical pain and spiritual suffering, Jesus is now in the last stage of death. How can he take it? Some people drift away from the gruesome ordeal. Others watch and wonder at the silence of the suffering servant. The crucified one is quiet for almost three hours.

Then the silence is broken. In a loud voice, Jesus cries out, *"Eloi, Eloi, lama sabachthanni?"* (Matthew 27:46). That's Aramaic. The English translation is "My God, my God, why have you forsaken me?" Some people nearby mistakenly say, "He's calling Elijah." In truth, he's calling God, using the words of Psalm 22.

> *My God, my God, why have you forsaken me?*
> *Why are you so far from helping me, from the words of*
>   *my groaning?*
> *O my God, I cry by day, but you do not answer; and by*
>   *night, but find no rest.*
> — Psalm 22:1-2 (NRSV)

In this prayer of desolation Jesus is quoting scriptures, but what does this cry of dereliction mean?

Saint Paul offers this interpretation: "God made him who had no sin to be sin for us, so that in him we might become the righteousness of God" (2 Corinthians 5:21). Sin alienates us from God. The sinless Jesus takes the sins of all people of all time upon himself and thus becomes the alienated one. In his sense of total isolation, feeling abandoned and alienated from his Father, Jesus drops into the hellish state called the *great ordeal.*

In order to better understand the *great ordeal*, and its meaning, it may be helpful to go back to the prayer Jesus taught his followers.

Our Father in heaven,
hallowed be your name,
your kingdom come,
your will be done on earth as it is in heaven.
Give us today our daily bread.
Forgive us our debts,
as we also have forgiven our debtors
and lead us not into temptation, but deliver us from the
   evil one.

— Matthew 6:9-13

John V. Taylor, a New Testament scholar, translates the last petition of the Lord's Prayer in a helpful way: "Save us from the *great ordeal* and deliver us from the evil one." Taylor connects the prayer petition to the cry of dereliction from the cross.

The great ordeal is the experience of the absence of God. Since Jesus ushered in the kingdom of God and begins his prayer with the term of affectionate intimacy, *Abba*, literally "Daddy" (which we translate "Father"), we might expect that there would be no interruption of this intimate relationship throughout his life.

Instead, we find Jesus hanging on the cross at the end of his earthly life and feeling totally, utterly forsaken by his *Abba*. In strange juxtaposition to the intimacy of the first word of the Lord's Prayer, behold alienation. On the cross we find Jesus praying in the midst of the *great ordeal* in his cry of dereliction and experiencing the apparent absence of God. Jesus' struggle and conflict with the evil one is real and profound throughout his life, but especially so as he hangs suspended between earth and heaven, crushed as the alienated one by the sins of the world. Behold the heart of darkness.

In the heart of darkness, Jesus feels God has deserted him. God who has always been his *Abba*, as close as the air he breathed, suddenly seems to disappear, leaving his Son in total despair, feeling depressed, deserted, devoid, and desolate — the *great ordeal*.

On that first Good Friday, Jesus carries the sins and burdens of all of us on his back at one point in time. He goes to the heart of hell — hopelessness — and faces it down. He enters utter darkness so that we need never go there. Jesus blazes the trail through the heart of darkness so that we can see the light of God's presence, even when it seems like God doesn't care. Jesus prays, "My God, my God, why have you forsaken me?" so that we need never swallow the demonic lure to give up on God. We can get through "the dark night of the soul" because Jesus went there and came out victorious.

From now on, as you pray the Lord's Prayer petition about the *great ordeal*, you step away from "puppy sins" and look straight into the eyes of the monster called the evil one. As you pray this petition, remember that on the cross Jesus went into the heart of darkness, got through it, and went on to victory. Thus, as you listen to the terrifying words "My God, my God, why have you forsaken me?" they become good news.

"I Am Thirsty"

As you hear Jesus' fifth word from the cross, "I am thirsty" (John 19:28b), remember Jesus is again quoting scripture.

> *Insults have broken my heart, so that I am in despair.*
> *I looked for pity, but there was none;*
> *and for comforters, but I found none.*
> *They gave me poison for food,*
> *and for my thirst they gave me vinegar to drink.*
> — Psalm 69:20-21 (NRSV)

We behold the humanity of Jesus. The same gospel that insists Jesus is the Great I Am and prefaces this remark about thirst by reminding us of Jesus' more than human remembrance, "knowing all scripture would be fulfilled" (John 19:28a), also insists we face the human aspect of Jesus' life and death. The bodily need for drink is the reminder that the Son of God is like us in every aspect, except sin (Hebrews 4:15). As we behold Jesus hanging there on the cross we are reminded that he is blood of our blood, bone of our bone, flesh of our flesh, our brother. That he was thirsty reminds us of his identification with our humanity.

Thirst is a major element in the terrible, torturing death by crucifixion. Charles Swindoll writes, "The mouths and throats of all victims hanging on crosses cried for water. The lips cracked and bled as the eyes glazed. The tongues swelled in the mouths and saliva hung like drying glue in the throats."[2]

"It Is Finished"

"When he had received the drink, Jesus said, 'It is finished' " (John 19:30).

As you stand at the foot of the cross, you don't hear this sixth word as an exhausted expression of a defeated man. No, listen again — his is a shout of victory. The New English Bible translation puts it this way: "It is accomplished!" In other words, "What you sent me to do, I have done. I have carried out the mission fully, even to the point of dying to fulfill the prophecies and meet human needs. Sin must be punished. I am *sin* personified. Mission accomplished."

"Completed. Finished. Paid in full. Accomplished."

Only God could accomplish the work of salvation. In the person of Jesus at the historical event called the crucifixion, Jesus does just that. He dies for all, that all might have the opportunity of life and salvation.

We don't accomplish salvation. We receive salvation as a gift. It's like a check for a million dollars, freely given to us by the Lord. We don't accomplish these riches. Our job is to appropriate what has been accomplished by turning the check over and signing it. We need to endorse the check. We need to personally appropriate what Jesus has accomplished on the cross.

"Father, Into Your Hands I Commit My Spirit"

Watch and listen to the final words of the Lord before his death. They are like a glorious sunset after a raging storm. The last statement of Jesus, the seventh word from the cross, brings us from the depths of Jesus' feeling betrayed and forsaken to the heights of personal intimacy once again. Jesus calls out with a loud voice, "Father [*Abba*], into your hands I commit my spirit" (Luke 23:46).

Once again, Jesus is praying as was his custom, *Abba*. As in life he prayed with every move he made, so here in death his last word is a prayer of commitment. Again quoting scriptures, this time Psalm 31:5a, Jesus dies on the cross as he had lived, in affectionate intimacy with his Father giving his life for us, committed to God's will.

The cross — listen, Jesus is speaking to you as if there were no one else on earth, "I'd rather die than give you up."

The cross — look at him there, calling for everyone to come to him and receive the free gift of eternal life he gives. Malcolm Muggeridge, the cynical British newscaster turned Christian late in life, says, "It is the cross more than anything else that has called me inexorably to Christ."

The cross — remember, Jesus promises, "I, when I am lifted up from the earth, will draw all men to myself" (John 12:32). Feel the magnetism of the uplifted Lord. The monk mentioned earlier in this chapter, held a large lit candle beneath the crucifix in the dark church and said, "Behold what has been done for you." Look up and live. "... The Son of Man must be lifted up, that everyone who believes in him may have eternal life" (John 3:14b-15).

Don't despair. Look at the man on the cross.

---

1. The seven sentences of Jesus from the cross are generally called "the seven last words of Christ."

2. Charles Swindoll, *The Darkness and the Dawn* (Nashville: Word, 2001), p. 181.

Questions For Your Personal Consideration And/Or Group Discussion

1. What is the meaning of the seven last "words" of Christ from the cross?

   a. "Father, forgive them for they don't know what they are doing" (Luke 23:34).
   b. "Today you will be with me in paradise" (Luke 23:43).
   c. "Dear woman, here is your son ... [John] here is your mother" (John 19:26b-27).
   d. "My God, my God, why have you forsaken me?" (Matthew 27:46).
   e. "I am thirsty" (John 19:28b).
   f. "It is finished" (John 19:30).
   g. "Father, into your hands I commit my spirit" (Luke 23:46).

2. What does the suffering and death of Jesus have to do with your suffering and death?

3. Read Colossians 3:12-14. What is the motivation for us forgiving one another?

4. Read Hebrews 4:14-16. How is Jesus "the great high priest"?

5. Read Philippians 2:5-12. What does it mean that Jesus "emptied himself" (Philippians 2:7 NRSV)?

6. Read Luke 23:44-45. What does the rending of the temple curtain mean?

7. First Corinthians 15:3 says, "For what I received I passed on to you as of first importance: that Christ died for your sins according to the scriptures...." Discuss some of the scriptures that are fulfilled at Christ's crucifixion:

   a. Isaiah 53:1-12
   b. Psalm 22:1-2 and 22:18
   c. Psalm 69:20-31
   d. Psalm 31:5a

Chapter 12

The Resurrection
And The Healing Of Memories

John 20:1-18; 21:15-25

If you stood at the bottom of the Grand Canyon and looked up, you would be overwhelmed and filled with awe. That's how I feel as I face the task of trying to illustrate John 20 and 21. This final section of *The Eagle* will deal with Mary Magdalene's experience of the resurrected Jesus and the appearance of Jesus on the beach where Peter's mind is healed. These are two of the most poignant scenes in human history. In both stories, we see tension rise to fever pitch. In both, we sense colossal reversals, emotions deeper than the sea. We also see change, which reaches across time to where we live. My words are too small to capture the wonder and power of these scenes.

There are subplots to these two stories, including the pitiful efforts of Pilate and the high priests to guard the tomb. That would be an interesting theme to pursue, but that's not the heart of the matter. The uneven first reaction of all the disciples to Jesus coming back from death deserves some attention, as does the resolution of Thomas' doubts, the prediction of the apostle John's death, and a hundred other sub-themes within the larger theme of Jesus' resurrection story. They could attract our attention, but that too would lead us off center. These sub-themes will have to wait for another time and place.

Here, we focus on Mary Magdalene's experience and Peter's healing of memories. Telling these stories in the present tense may help to make them more real.

Mary And The Resurrected One

Let's look at Mary's experience in three parts: Jesus' use of Mary's name, Mary's personal response, and Mary's witnessing ministry.

First, we'll look at the spiritual power of Jesus' use of the personal name, "Mary." Planning to anoint Jesus' body that first Easter dawn, Mary goes to the tomb, only to find the great stone rolled away. Thinking that someone has stolen the body, she is frightened, confused, and brokenhearted. She runs to tell the other disciples who are gathered in the upper room of John Mark's house. "They have taken the Lord out of the tomb, and we don't know where they have put him," she screams at Peter and John (John 20:2).

Peter and John run to the tomb, only to discover that Jesus isn't there. The linen cloth that had covered Jesus' dead body is there, but the body is gone. Peter and John run back to tell the others.

Mary Magdalene stands outside the tomb crying. Then she looks into the tomb. She sees two strange figures dressed in white, seated where Jesus' body had been, one at the head and one at the foot. "Why are you crying?" they ask. "Who are you looking for?"

"They have taken my Lord away," she says, "and I don't know where they have put him" (John 20:13). Sadly, filled with grief and worry, she turns to leave. She sees a man standing nearby, but she doesn't recognize him. Her head is drooping, her eyes are red and swollen and filled with tears. She thinks the man is the gardener.

Then the man says, "Woman, why are you crying? Who are you looking for?"

"Sir, if you have carried him away, tell me where you have put him, and I will get him" (John 20:15). At this point, she is still thinking about the ritual anointing of the dead body.

A total reversal comes in one word — her name. "Mary," Jesus says. That changes everything. How often she had heard her name called by the Savior. How often he had called her to tell her some great truth. How often he had spoken her name because he wanted to remind her of the freedom he had given her when he called out seven demons, which had possessed her (Luke 8:2). All of this rushes through her mind. The incredible thing Jesus predicted has actually happened.

This is Jesus. He is back. He is alive. He is real. All of this is conveyed in that one word, "Mary." Behold the power of Jesus speaking Mary's name.

Mary Magdalene had found meaning for her life when Jesus healed her inner divisions. She had purpose as she followed him as one of his disciples. When he died she was devastated. Now, he is back. Once again he is calling her by name. There is power in this graveside reunion. What difference does this make for us today?

Like Mary, we are called by name. Like Mary, we are astounded to discover that we are personally known to our Lord. Like Mary, we enter the *great reversal* when we hear Jesus call us by name and experience the power of the personal.

A child made a salutary mistake while praying the Lord's Prayer: "Our Father, who art in heaven, how do you know my name?" Like this child, we wonder how God could possibly know us by name. We are amazed when we hear Jesus say things like, "... The very hairs of your head are all numbered" (Matthew 10:30). Jesus knows us.

A pastor was making his rounds one day. He wanted to meet the families in his new church. As he sat and sipped coffee, he asked the mother of the house, "How many children do you have?" She started to reply, "There's Johnny, he's the oldest; and Betty, the youngest; and Jimmy and...." The pastor interrupted her, "I just want their number, not their names." Crisply, the mother replied, "They don't have numbers. They have names." Exactly. The mother was right; the pastor wrong. The power of the personal is demonstrated by the use of names.

Second, the power of the personal continues on another level as we hear the post-resurrection story of Mary in the gospel of John. Note the power of personal response as we hear Mary respond to Jesus, *"Rabboni!"* (John 20:16b).

Rabboni is an Aramaic term. Aramaic is a dialect of Hebrew, the language usually used by Jesus. *Rabboni* is the title for Jesus, used by the disciples. It literally means, "teacher" or "master." The New English Bible translation is "my master."

Mary was a disciple of Jesus. Disciple means "follower." Jesus is the teacher and master for his followers. They call him "Lord." They live under his authority. Later, Thomas, the doubter, seeing the resurrected Jesus, cries out, "My Lord and my God!" (John 20:28). That's the Christian creed.

The power of a personal response to Jesus' authority over our lives continues in our day. The first Christian creed is, "Jesus is Lord." As we begin the Christian journey, we are invited to make the confession, "Jesus is my Lord and Savior." In the *Small Catechism*, Luther summarizes the meaning of the second article of the Apostles' Creed by beginning, "I believe that Jesus Christ — true God, Son of the Father from eternity, and true man, born of the Virgin Mary — is my Lord."[1]

That Jesus is *the* Lord is true enough, but not big enough. Larger. Make it larger. Jesus is *our* Lord is the biblical corrective for a distorted individualism, but this title is still lacking something. To confess "Jesus is *my* Lord" is the enlargement needed to make the personal connection with the master.

Personally living under the lordship of Christ means seeking to submit our wills to God's will. That's the one thing necessary and the hardest thing of all. Mary Magdalene's confession, "*Rabboni,*" is an acknowledgment that we can't run our own lives. We need a master, a teacher, a Lord. Our choice is not whether or not someone or something will rule over us, but only what or who will rule. As one person put it,

> *Unless that which is above you*
> *controls that which is within you,*
> *that which is around you will.*

> — Anonymous

John 20:16 offers us the spiritual power of both the use of the personal name by Jesus and the personal response of coming under the lordship of the resurrected Savior. In addition, this mind-expanding story offers us an example of the power of personal witnessing. Mary goes to the disciples with the news, "I have seen the Lord" (John 20:18). That's powerful, personal witnessing. Like Mary, we are called to witness for the resurrected one. This witness is necessary, but it isn't easy.

The apostles hear of the resurrection from Mary Magdalene (and the other women who found the tomb empty). They don't believe the women, because their words seem to them like nonsense (Luke 24:11) or as another translation puts it, "the words seemed to them an idle tale" (NRSV).

Mary Magdalene teaches us the way of personal witnessing. People who hear the good news of the gospel and the resurrection of Christ don't always respond positively. Some never respond positively and embrace the faith; others like the apostles, accept the resurrected one, but at a later time than we expect. We are called to be witnesses, but that just means planting seeds, not necessarily seeing the harvest.

It is not our job as Christians to make others believe in the resurrected Lord on our time schedule. It is our job to witness, like Mary Magdalene.

It is not our job to convince someone of the truths of God, just to witness.

It is not our job to convert anyone. The Holy Spirit does that. It is our calling to witness to people for Christ.[2]

Russ Stevenson of the American Mission in Alexandria said, "It is the essence of Christianity that it must be passed on. Just to receive Jesus and never pass him on to others is unthinkable. We are channels of the water of life, not pools." We are given the water of life so that we might pass this living water on to others.

Some years ago I was privileged to see the Oberammergau Passion Play. I was especially moved by the last scene where Mary Magdalene meets the resurrected Jesus. "Mary," he says. "*Rabboni*," she replies. Then Mary comes to the edge of the stage and pleads with us, the audience, to go and tell others, "Jesus is alive. I've seen him. Everyone must be told. They must know the good news."

That's witnessing. I'll never forget it.

The story of the resurrection is the heart of Christianity. The appearance of the resurrected Lord on the beach is an important extension to this story.

Peter's Healing Of Memories

The gospel of John reports the appearance of the resurrected Jesus in the upper room on Easter evening (when Thomas was absent) and again a week later (when Thomas was present). Chapter 21 of the fourth gospel reports that between these appearances and Christ's ascension into heaven, a soul-stirring event took place.

Peter, Thomas, Nathanael, James, John, and two other disciples decide to go fishing. While they are waiting for Jesus to tell them what to do next, they decide to follow their vocation. They go fishing, but they get "skunked." They fish all night, but don't catch a single fish. Discouraged, they head toward shore.

A stranger on the shore calls out, suggesting that they throw out their nets on the other side of the boat. There they catch so many fish they are unable to haul the net into the boat. John turns to shore and shouts, "It's the Lord." Peter dives into the water and swims ashore. The others in the boat drag the net ashore.

The reunited group sits around the fire and eats some of the fish. When they finish eating, Jesus suddenly turns to Peter and says, "Simon, son of John, do you truly love me more than these?" A shocking question out of nowhere. What does it mean? Why is he asking this question.

"Yes, Lord," Peter says, "you know that I love you."

Jesus says, "Feed my lambs."

Again Jesus says, "Simon, son of John, do you truly love me?"

If you were Peter, wouldn't you feel awkward at the first question and insulted by the second?

Squirming, Peter replies, "Yes, Lord, you know that I love you." *What's going on here?* Peter thinks. *I don't like the way he's talking to me.*

"Then take care of my sheep."

After an awkward silence, Jesus asks a third time, "Simon son of John, do you love me?"

The old anger begins to rage inside the big fisherman. Peter was hurt because Jesus asked him the third time, "Do you love me?" (John 21:17a). Who wouldn't be hurt by this kind of questioning from a friend?

Trying to contain the rage within, Peter responds, "Lord, you know all things; you know that I love you."

Jesus says evenly, "Feed my sheep."

Peter's threefold denial is being "undone" with three pointed questions and answers. To make Peter an effective witness, Jesus heals Peter's memories of his weak and demonic denials. If Peter is to become a "stand up" witness for the Lord, forgiveness as a personal reality had to take place. The sting of memories can be our undoing. What difference does Peter's story make for us today?

A secular author has suggested, "Memories have no mercy." This author picked up on a half truth. From a human point of view, memories of our sins, our disobedience, and our cowardly acts haunt us. Bad memories of what we have done or what we perceive others have done to us seemingly have no mercy. They keep us from proper sleep. They affect the way we treat other people. What the secular author missed is that with Christ, bad memories can be healed by forgiveness. That's what is happening in our story. That's the message of the questions on the beach for us today.

Like Peter, there are things in our minds that prevent us from being effective witnesses. There are secret sins and haunting memories that bog us down, drag us backward, and keep us from being free to go forward. Secrets make us sick. Like Peter, we have our denials, sins, and times of cowardly thoughts and actions. Often we have missed opportunities to speak for the Lord because of bad memories. We have had

- times when we could have stood up for Christ, but didn't;
- times when we were quiet when we should have witnessed when it was uncomfortable so we chose the easy way out;
- times when we spoke amiss because we didn't have the courage of our convictions;

- times of anger and resentment that haunt us; and
- times when memories that seem to have no mercy were in control.

Like Peter, we need forgiveness for our sins. We, too, need freedom from bad memories. We, too, need to have our minds cleared of those times we feel we have been mistreated, cornered, or misunderstood. We too need to be freed from the past so that we can go forward with our lives.

Like Peter, we need the healing of memories. Like Peter, we can be healed by the Lord Jesus Christ.

We pick up Peter's story in verse 18 of John 21. "I tell you the truth, when you were younger you dressed yourself and went where you wanted; but when you are old you will stretch out your hands, and someone else will dress you and lead you where you do not want to go. 'Follow me.' "

As a result of being healed, Peter becomes a great witness for the Lord. Chapter 2 of Acts reports Peter's bold sermon to a hostile crowd on Pentecost.

> *Therefore, let all Israel be assured of this: God has made this Jesus, whom you crucified, both Lord and Christ. When the people heard this, they were cut to the heart and said to Peter and the other apostles, "Brothers, what shall we do?"*
>
> *Peter replied, "Repent and be baptized, every one of you, in the name of Jesus Christ for the forgiveness of your sins. And you will receive the gift of the Holy Spirit...."*
>
> *With many other words he warned them; and he pleaded with them, "Save yourselves from this corrupt generation." Those who accepted his message were baptized, and about three thousand were added to their number that day.* — Acts 2:36-41

Freed from the sting of his denials, Peter preached boldly. He also spoke boldly to Jewish officials when they had him arrested for preaching Christ and healing a cripple in the name of Jesus.

Before the Sanhedrin, the Jewish supreme court that had condemned Jesus, Peter was asked, "By what power or what name did you do this?" (Acts 4:7). Peter's bold answer shocked the court.

> Then Peter, filled with the Holy Spirit, said to them, "Rulers and elders of the people! If we are being called to account today for an act of kindness shown to a cripple and are asked how he was healed, then know this, you and all the people of Israel: It is by the name of Jesus Christ of Nazareth, whom you crucified but whom God raised from the dead, that this man stands before you healed....
> "Salvation is found in no one else, for there is no other name under heaven given to men by which we must be saved."   — Acts 4:8-12

The reaction of the rulers provides insight into the healing Jesus had given to Peter's heart in the beach encounter.

> When they saw the courage of Peter and John and realized that they were unschooled, ordinary men, they were astonished and they took note that these men had been with Jesus.   — Acts 4:13

Tradition says that in his final arrest for being a Christian, Peter was threatened with crucifixion. Peter boldly declared that he was not worthy to be crucified in the same position as his Lord. His request to be crucified upside down was granted, fulfilling Jesus' prediction that the day would come when he was older and wiser when his hands would be stretched out and he would be led to where he did not want to go.

The story of Peter reaches across time and touches our hearts today. The resurrected Jesus heals our memories today, just as he did with Peter long ago.

In his book, *Crying For My Mother*,[3] Wesley Nelson tells of the healing of his memories, which inhibited his ministry. Noticing that as a boy Wesley "clung to his mother's apron strings," his father tried to make his son grow up and be a man by telling Wesley that his mother had gone away for good. In fact, she had gone out of town for a short time. The father was trying to make Wesley face life without always crying for his mother, but the incident made an indelible mark on the boy's mind. His mother came back, took him in her arms, and talked softly with him as she had done before, but he never accepted her back emotionally.

For fifty years, when loss or grief or crisis came, Wesley had the same frantic feeling of loss and emptiness he had felt that day. "I felt like a misfit," he said with pathos, recalling how his little self-image had been damaged when people laughed at him or ridiculed him when he cried as a boy.

Wesley went through a conversion experience. Soon thereafter, he went into the ministry of the Covenant church. He knew there was an unresolved alienation in his heart but couldn't change the feeling of being a misfit. He was a good pastor. He did graduate work and rose to the level of professor at a seminary. He wrote books. Still, haunting memories inhibited him.

On a speaking engagement, he gave a talk, which the audience greatly appreciated. Afterward, several women came up to him, thanked him, and hugged him. At first, this greatly confused him because he was in a conservative and strict denomination that warned that contact between the sexes could lead to lustful temptations and downfall. He prayed about what had happened to him when the women hugged him. Suddenly, it dawned on him that God had used the women to undo the memories, which haunted him. This sixty-year-old man finally realized the hugs had healed him. Like Peter, Wesley was freed to be a better witness for Christ.

Mary and Peter reach across time and tell us that we too can be freed from fear and bad memories by the resurrected one.

These poor words of mine fall far short of telling the whole story. "Don't despair," they say. I still hear the Lord saying, "Ron, make it larger. You haven't told the half of it."

I am comforted by the words of the apostle John who felt the same way when he wrote and told his account of the good news of Jesus, the resurrection, and the healing of memories.

Jesus did many other things as well. If every one of them were written down, I suppose that even the whole world would not have room for the books that would be written.   — John 21:25

---

1. Martin Luther, *The Small Catechism* (Minneapolis: Augsburg Fortress, 1979), p. 13.

2. For further information about witnessing, see Ron Lavin, *Witness: The Reign of God and Missional Churches Today* (Lima, Ohio: CSS Publishing Company, Inc., 2007).

3. Wesley Nelson, *Crying for My Mother* (Chicago: Covenant Press, 1975).

Questions For Your Personal Consideration
And/Or Group Discussion

1. Why is it important for a pastor to call church members by name?

2. How would you describe the reversal in Mary Magdalene when she heard her name called (John 20:16a)?

3. Why is Mary's personal response "*Rabboni*" (teacher) important to us today (John 20:16b)?

4. Comment on the poem:

    Unless that which above you
    controls that which is within you,
    that which is around you will.

                                    — Anonymous

5. What do these two stories have to do with our suffering and temptations to feel despair?

6. Read 2 Corinthians 10:3-5. How do Christians wage war in different ways than the world?

7. Read John 21:15-19. How does this story of Peter apply to us today?

8. Read Acts 2:36-41. Compare Peter's cowardly behavior in the high priest's courtyard with this bold sermon.

9. What do you make of the significance that when Peter was martyred he refused to be crucified in the same position as his Lord? He was crucified upside down.

www.ingramcontent.com/pod-product-compliance
Lightning Source LLC
LaVergne TN
LVHW051641080426
835511LV00016B/2430